Marx Machiavelli Chesterton Emerson Joyce Abbott Hardy Montaigne Cooper Austen Defoe Melville Haggard Hugo Christie Carroll Eliot Grimm Stoker Molière Wilde Maupassant Byron Schiller Engels Garnett Einstein Fitzgerald Smith Goethe Hawthorne Kafka Cotton Dostoyevsky Hall Baum Kipling Doyle Willis Leslie Dumas Henry Nietzsche Flaubert Turgenev Balzac Stockton Vatsyayana Crane Burroughs Whitman Verne Curtis Tocqueville Gogol Vinci Homer Widger Tolstoy Busch Darwin Thoreau Scott Potter Freud Zola Twain Plato Lawrence Kant Jowett Stevenson Dickens Andersen Burton Hesse Harte London Descartes Cervantes Poe Aristotle Wells Voltaire Hale James Hastings Cooke Bunner Shakespeare Richter Chambers Irving Doré Chekhov da Shaw Wodehouse Benedict Alcott Swift Dante Pushkin Newton tredition®

tredition was established in 2006 by Sandra Latusseck and Soenke Schulz. Based in Hamburg, Germany, tredition offers publishing solutions to authors and publishing houses, combined with worldwide distribution of printed and digital book content. tredition is uniquely positioned to enable authors and publishing houses to create books on their own terms and without conventional manufacturing risks.

For more information please visit: www.tredition.com

TREDITION CLASSICS

This book is part of the TREDITION CLASSICS series. The creators of this series are united by passion for literature and driven by the intention of making all public domain books available in printed format again - worldwide. Most TREDITION CLASSICS titles have been out of print and off the bookstore shelves for decades. At tredition we believe that a great book never goes out of style and that its value is eternal. Several mostly non-profit literature projects provide content to tredition. To support their good work, tredition donates a portion of the proceeds from each sold copy. As a reader of a TREDITION CLASSICS book, you support our mission to save many of the amazing works of world literature from oblivion. See all available books at www.tredition.com.

Project Gutenberg

The content for this book has been graciously provided by Project Gutenberg. Project Gutenberg is a non-profit organization founded by Michael Hart in 1971 at the University of Illinois. The mission of Project Gutenberg is simple: To encourage the creation and distribution of eBooks. Project Gutenberg is the first and largest collection of public domain eBooks.

Problems of Expansion As Considered In Papers and Addresses

Whitelaw Reid

Imprint

This book is part of TREDITION CLASSICS

Author: Whitelaw Reid
Cover design: Buchgut, Berlin – Germany

Publisher: tredition GmbH, Hamburg - Germany
ISBN: 978-3-8472-1811-1

www.tredition.com
www.tredition.de

The intention of the TREDITION CLASSICS series is to make world literature in the public domain available in printed format. Literary enthusiasts and organizations, such as Project Gutenberg, worldwide have scanned and digitally edited the original texts. tredition has subsequently formatted and redesigned the content into a modern reading layout. Therefore, we cannot guarantee the exact reproduction of the original format of a particular historic edition. Please also note that no modifications have been made to the spelling, therefore it may differ from the orthography used today.

PROBLEMS OF EXPANSION

AS CONSIDERED IN PAPERS AND ADDRESSES

BY

WHITELAW REID

NEW YORK
THE CENTURY CO.
1900

THE DEVINNE PRESS.

PREFATORY NOTE

So general have been the expressions as to the value of these scattered papers and addresses that I have thought it a useful service to gather them together from the authorized publications at the time, or, in some cases, from newspaper reports, and (with the consent of the Century Co. and of Mr. John Lane for the copyrighted articles) to embody them consecutively, in the order of their several dates, in this volume.

The article entitled "The Territory with which We are Threatened" was prepared before the appointment of its author as a member of the Commission to negotiate terms of peace with Spain, and published only a few days afterward. This circumstance attracted unusual attention to its views about retaining the territory the country had taken.

As to the attitude of every one else connected officially with the determination of that question there has been, naturally, more or less diplomatic reserve; but the position of Mr. Reid before he was appointed was thus clearly revealed. When the storm of opposition was apparently reaching its height, in June, 1899, he took occasion to avow explicitly the course it was obvious he must have recommended. In his address at the Seventy-fifth Anniversary of Miami University, referring to some apparently authorized despatches on the subject from Washington, he said: "I readily take the time which hostile critics consider unfavorable, for accepting my own share of responsibility, and for avowing for myself that I declared my belief in the duty and policy of holding the whole Philippine Archipelago in the very first conference of the Commissioners in the President's room at the White House, in advance of any instructions of any sort. If vindication for it be needed, I confidently await the future."

This measure of responsibility for the expansion policy upon which the country is launched has necessarily given special interest to Mr. Reid's subsequent discussions of the various problems it has raised. They have been called for on important occasions both abroad and in all parts of our own country. They have covered many phases of the subject, but have preserved a singular uniformity of purpose and consistency of ideas throughout. They appeared at times when public men often seemed to be groping in the dark on an unknown road, but it is now evident that the road which has been taken is substantially the road they marked out. As a foreign critic said in comment on one of the addresses: "The author is one man who knows what he thinks about the new policy required by the new situation in which his country is placed, and has the courage and candor to say it."

It has seemed desirable with each paper and address to prefix a brief record of the circumstances under which it was made. A few memoranda which Mr. Reid had prepared to elucidate the text are added, in foot-notes and in the Appendices which include the Resolutions of Congress as to Cuba, the Protocol of Washington, and the text of the Peace of Paris.

C. C. Buel.

New Rochelle, New York,
May 25, 1900.

I

THE TERRITORY WITH WHICH WE ARE THREATENED

This paper first appeared in "The Century Magazine" for September, 1898, for which it was written some time before the author's appointment as a member of the Paris Commission to negotiate the terms of peace with Spain, and, in fact, before hostilities had been suspended or the peace protocol agreed upon in Washington.

THE TERRITORY WITH WHICH WE ARE THREATENED

Men are everywhere asking what should be our course about the territory conquered in this war. Some inquire merely if it is good policy for the United States to abandon its continental limitations, and extend its rule over semi-tropical countries with mixed populations. Others ask if it would not be the wisest policy to give them away after conquering them, or abandon them. They say it would be ruinous to admit them as States to equal rights with ourselves, and contrary to the Constitution to hold them permanently as Territories. It would be bad policy, they argue, to lower the standard of our population by taking in hordes of West Indians and Asiatics; bad policy to run any chance of allowing these people to become some day joint arbiters with ourselves of the national destinies; bad policy to abandon the principles of Washington's Farewell Address, to which we have adhered for a century, and involve ourselves in the Eastern question, or in the entanglements of European politics.

The men who raise these questions are sincere and patriotic. They are now all loyally supporting the Government in the prosecution of the war which some of them were active in bringing on, and others to the last deprecated and resisted. Their doubts and difficulties deserve the fairest consideration, and are of pressing importance.

Duty First, not Policy.

But is there not another question, more important, which first demands consideration? Have we the right to decide whether we shall hold or abandon the conquered territory, solely, or even mainly as a matter of national policy? Are we not bound by our own acts, and by the responsibility we have voluntarily assumed before Spain, before Europe, and before the civilized world, to consider it first in the light of national duty?

For that consideration it is not needful now to raise the question whether we were in every particular justifiable for our share in the transactions leading to the war. However men's opinions on that point may differ, the Nation is now at war for a good cause, and has in a vigorous prosecution of it the loyal and zealous support of all good citizens.

The President intervened, with our Army and Navy, under the direct command of Congress, to put down Spanish rule in Cuba, on the distinct ground that it was a rule too bad to be longer endured. Are we not, then, bound in honor and morals to see to it that the government which replaces Spanish rule is better? Are we not morally culpable and disgraced before the civilized world if we leave it as bad or worse? Can any consideration of mere policy, of our own interests, or our own ease and comfort, free us from that solemn responsibility which we have voluntarily assumed, and for which we have lavishly spilled American and Spanish blood?

Most people now realize from what a mistake Congress was kept by the firm attitude of the President in opposing a recognition of the so-called Cuban Republic of Cubitas. It is now generally understood that virtually there was no Cuban Republic, or any Cuban government save that of wandering bands of guerrilla insurgents, probably less numerous and influential than had been represented. There seems reason to believe that however bad Spanish government may have been, the rule of these people, where they had the power, was as bad; and still greater reason to apprehend that if they had full power, their sense of past wrongs and their unrestrained tropical thirst for vengeance might lead to something worse. Is it for that pitiful result that a civilized and Christian people is giving up its sons and pouring out blood and treasure in Cuba?

In commanding the war, Congress pledged us to continue our action until the pacification of the island should be secured. When that happy time has arrived, if it shall then be found that the Cuban insurgents and their late enemies are able to unite in maintaining a settled and peaceable government in Cuba, distinctly free from the faults which now lead the United States to destroy the old one, we shall have discharged our responsibility, and will be at liberty to end our interference. But if not, the responsibility of the United

States continues. It is morally bound to secure to Cuba such a government, even if forced by circumstances to furnish it itself.

The Pledge of Congress.

At this point, however, we are checked by a reminder of the further action of Congress, "asserting its determination, when the pacification of Cuba has been accomplished, to leave the government and control of the island to its people."

Now, the secondary provisions of any great measure must be construed in the light of its main purpose; and where they conflict, we are led to presume that they would not have been adopted but for ignorance of the actual conditions. Is it not evident that such was the case here? We now know how far Congress was misled as to the organization and power of the alleged Cuban government, the strength of the revolt, and the character of the war the insurgents were waging. We have seen how little dependence could be placed upon the lavish promises of support from great armies of insurgents in the war we have undertaken; and we are beginning to realize the difference between our idea of a humane and civilized "pacification" and that apparently entertained up to this time by the insurgents. It is certainly true that when the war began neither Congress nor the people of the United States cherished an intention to hold Cuba permanently, or had any further thought than to pacify it and turn it over to its own people. But they must pacify it before they turn it over; and, from present indications, to do that thoroughly may be the work of years. Even then they are still responsible to the world for the establishment of a better government than the one they destroy. If the last state of that island should be worse than the first, the fault and the crime must be solely that of the United States. We were not actually forced to involve ourselves; we might have passed by on the other side. When, instead, we insisted on interfering, we made ourselves responsible for improving the situation; and, no matter what Congress "disclaimed," or what intention it "asserted," we cannot leave Cuba till that is done without national dishonor and blood-guiltiness.

Egypt and Cuba.

The situation is curiously like that of England in Egypt. She intervened too, under far less provocation, it must be admitted, and for a cause rather more commercial than humanitarian. But when some thought that her work was ended and that it was time for her to go, Lord Granville, on behalf of Mr. Gladstone's government, addressed the other great European Powers in a note on the outcome of which Congress might have reflected with profit before framing its resolutions. "Although for the present," he said, "a British force remains in Egypt for the preservation of public tranquillity, Her Majesty's government are desirous of withdrawing it as soon as the state of the country and the organization of proper means for the maintenance of the Khedive's authority will admit of it. In the meantime the position in which Her Majesty's government are placed towards His Highness imposes upon them the duty of giving advice, with the object of securing that the order of things to be established shall be of a satisfactory character and possess the elements of stability and progress." As time went on this declaration did not seem quite explicit enough; and accordingly, just a year later, Lord Granville instructed the present Lord Cromer, then Sir Evelyn Baring, that it should be made clear to the Egyptian ministers and governors of provinces that "the responsibility which for the time rests on England obliges Her Majesty's government to insist on the adoption of the policy which they recommend, and that it will be necessary that those ministers and governors who do not follow this course should cease to hold their offices."

That was in 1884—a year after the defeat of Arabi, and the "pacification." It is now fourteen years later. The English are still there, and the Egyptian ministers and governors now understand quite well that they must cease to hold their offices if they do not adopt the policy recommended by the British diplomatic agent. If it should be found that we cannot with honor and self-respect begin to abandon our self-imposed task of Cuban "pacification" with any greater speed, the impetuous congressmen, as they read over their own inconsiderate resolutions fourteen years hence, can hide their blushes behind a copy of Lord Granville's letter. They may explain, if they like, with the classical excuse of Benedick, "When I said I would die a bachelor, I did not think I should live till I were married." Or if this seems too frivolous for their serious plight, let them recall the position of Mr. Jefferson, who originally declared that the purchase of foreign territory would make waste paper of the Constitution, and subsequently appealed to Congress for the money to pay for his purchase of Louisiana. When he held such an acquisition unconstitutional, he had not thought he would live to want Louisiana.

As to Cuba, it may be fairly concluded that only these points are actually clear: (1) We had made ourselves in a sense responsible for Spain's rule in that island by our consistent declaration, through three quarters of a century, that no other European nation should replace her—Daniel Webster, as Secretary of State, even seeking to guard her hold as against Great Britain. (2) We are now at war because we say Spanish rule is intolerable; and we cannot withdraw our hand till it is replaced by a rule for which we are willing to be responsible. (3) We are also pledged to remain till the pacification is complete.

The Conquered Territories.

In the other territories in question the conditions are different. We are not taking possession of them, as we are of Cuba, with the avowed purpose of giving them a better government. We are conquering them because we are at war with Spain, which has been holding and governing them very much as she has Cuba; and we must strike Spain wherever and as hard as we can. But it must at once be recognized that as to Porto Rico at least, to hold it would be the natural course and what all the world would expect. Both Cuba and Porto Rico, like Hawaii, are within the acknowledged sphere of our influence, and ours must necessarily be the first voice in deciding their destiny. Our national position with regard to them is historic. It has been officially declared and known to every civilized nation for three quarters of a century. To abandon it now, that we may refuse greatness through a sudden craven fear of being great, would be so astonishing a reversal of a policy steadfastly maintained by the whole line of our responsible statesmen since 1823 as to be grotesque.

John Quincy Adams, writing in April of that year, as Secretary of State, to our Minister to Spain, pointed out that the dominion of Spain upon the American continents, North and South, was irrevocably gone, but warned him that Cuba and Porto Rico still remained nominally dependent upon her, and that she might attempt to transfer them. That could not be permitted, as they were "natural appendages to the North American continent." Subsequent statements turned more upon what Mr. Adams called "the transcendent importance of Cuba to the United States"; but from that day to this I do not recall a line in our state papers to show that the claim of the United States to control the future of Porto Rico as well as of Cuba was ever waived. As to Cuba, Mr. Adams predicted that within half a century its annexation would be indispensable. "There are laws of political as well as of physical gravitation," he said; and "Cuba, forcibly disjoined from its own unnatural connection with Spain, and incapable of self-support, can gravitate only towards the North American Union, which, by the same law of nature, cannot cast her off from its bosom." If Cuba is incapable of self-support, and could not therefore be left, in the cheerful language of Congress, to her own people, how much less could little Porto Rico stand alone?

There remains the alternative of giving Porto Rico back to Spain at the end of the war. But if we are warranted now in making war because the character of Spanish rule in Cuba was intolerable, how could we justify ourselves in handing back Porto Rico to the same rule, after having once emancipated her from it? The subject need not be pursued. To return Porto Rico to Spain, after she is once in our possession, is as much beyond the power of the President and of Congress as it was to preserve the peace with Spain after the destruction of the *Maine* in the harbor of Havana. From that moment the American people resolved that the flag under which this calamity was possible should disappear forever from the Western hemisphere, and they will sanction no peace that permits it to remain.

The question of the Philippines is different and more difficult. They are not within what the diplomatists of the world would recognize as the legitimate sphere of American influence. Our relation to them is purely the accident of recent war. We are not in honor bound to hold them, if we can honorably dispose of them. But we know that their grievances differ only in kind, not in degree, from those of Cuba; and having once freed them from the Spanish yoke, we cannot honorably require them to go back under it again. That would be to put us in an attitude of nauseating national hypocrisy; to give the lie to all our professions of humanity in our interference in Cuba, if not also to prove that our real motive was conquest. What humanity forbade us to tolerate in the West Indies, it would not justify us in reëstablishing in the Philippines.

What, then, can we do with them? Shall we trade them for something nearer home? Doubtless that would be permissible, if we were sure of thus securing them a better government than that of Spain, and if it could be done without precipitating fresh international difficulties. But we cannot give them to our friend and their neighbor Japan without instantly provoking the hostility of Russia, which recently interfered to prevent a far smaller Japanese aggrandizement. We cannot give them to Russia without a greater injustice to Japan; or to Germany or to France or to England without raising far more trouble than we allay. England would like us to keep them; the Continental nations would like that better than any other control excepting Spain's or their own; and the Philippines would prefer it to anything save the absolute independence which they are incapable of maintaining. Having been led into their possession by the course of a war undertaken for the sake of humanity, shall we draw a geographical limit to our humanity, and say we cannot continue to be governed by it in Asiatic waters because it is too much trouble and is too disagreeable—and, besides, there may be no profit in it?

Both war and diplomacy have many surprises; and it is quite possible that some way out of our embarrassing possession may yet be found. The fact is clear that many of our people do not much want it; but if a way of relinquishing it is proposed, the one thing we are bound to insist on is that it shall be consistent with our attitude in the war, and with our honorable obligations to the islands we have conquered and to civilization.

Fear of them as States.

The chief aversion to the vast accessions of territory with which we are threatened springs from the fear that ultimately they must be admitted into the Union as States. No public duty is more urgent at this moment than to resist from the very outset the concession of such a possibility. In no circumstances likely to exist within a century should they be admitted as States of the Union. The loose, disunited, and unrelated federation of independent States to which this would inevitably lead, stretching from the Indian Archipelago to the Caribbean Sea, embracing all climes, all religions, all races,—black, yellow, white, and their mixtures,—all conditions, from pagan ignorance and the verge of cannibalism to the best product of centuries of civilization, education, and self-government, all with equal rights in our Senate and representation according to population in our House, with an equal voice in shaping our national destinies—that would, at least in this stage of the world, be humanitarianism run mad, a degeneration and degradation of the homogeneous, continental Republic of our pride too preposterous for the contemplation of serious and intelligent men. Quite as well might Great Britain now invite the swarming millions of India to send rajas and members of the lower House, in proportion to population, to swamp the Lords and Commons and rule the English people. If it had been supposed that even Hawaii, with its overwhelming preponderance of Kanakas and Asiatics, would become a State, she could not have been annexed. If the territories we are conquering must become States, we might better renounce them at once and place them under the protectorate of some humane and friendly European Power with less nonsense in its blood.

This is not to deny them the freest and most liberal institutions they are capable of sustaining. The people of Sitka and the Aleutian Islands enjoy the blessings of ordered liberty and free institutions, but nobody dreams of admitting them to Statehood. New Mexico has belonged to us for half a century, not only without oppression, but with all the local self-government for which she was prepared; yet, though an integral part of our continent, surrounded by States, and with an adequate population, she is still not admitted to Statehood. Why should not the people on the island of Porto Rico, or even of Cuba, prosper and be happy for the next century under a rule similar in the main to that under which their kinsmen of New Mexico have prospered for the last half-century?

With some necessary modifications, the territorial form of government which we have tried so successfully from the beginning of the Union is well adapted to the best of such communities. It secures local self-government, equality before the law, upright courts, ample power for order and defense, and such control by Congress as gives security against the mistakes or excesses of people new to the exercise of these rights.

Will the Constitution Permit Withholding Statehood?

But such a system, we are told, is contrary to our Constitution and to the spirit of our institutions. Why? We have had just that system ever since the Constitution was framed. It is true that a large part of the territory thus governed has now been admitted into the Union in the form of new States. But it is not true that this was recognized at the beginning as a right, or even generally contemplated as a probability; nor is it true that it has been the purpose or expectation of those who annexed foreign territory to the United States, like the Louisiana or the Gadsden Purchase, that it would all be carved into States. That feature of the marvelous development of the continent has come as a surprise to this generation and the last, and would have been absolutely incredible to the men of Thomas Jefferson's time. Obviously, then, it could not have been the purpose for which, before that date, our territorial system was devised. It is not clear that the founders of the Government expected even all the territory we possessed at the outset to be made into States. Much of it was supposed to be worthless and uninhabitable. But it is certain that they planned for outside accessions. Even in the Articles of Confederation they provided for the admission of Canada and of British colonies which included Jamaica as well as Nova Scotia. Madison, in referring to this, construes it as meaning that they contemplated only the admission of these colonies as colonies, not the eventual establishment of new States ("Federalist," No. 43). About the same time Hamilton was dwelling on the alarms of those who thought the country already too large, and arguing that great size was a safeguard against ambitious rulers.

Nevertheless, the objectors still argue, the Constitution gives no positive warrant for a permanent territorial policy. But it does! Ordinarily it may be assumed that what the framers of the Constitution immediately proceeded to do under it was intended by them to be warranted by it; and we have seen that they immediately devised and maintained a territorial system for the government of territory which they had no expectation of ever converting into States. The case, however, is even plainer than that. The sole reference in the Constitution to the territories of the United States is in Article IV, Section 3: "The Congress shall have power to dispose of and make all needful rules and regulations respecting the territory or other property belonging to the United States." Jefferson revised his first views far enough to find warrant for acquiring territory; but here is explicit, unmistakable authority conferred for dealing with it, and with other "property," precisely as Congress chooses. The territory was not a present or prospective party in interest in the Union created under this organic act. It was "property," to be disposed of or ruled and regulated as Congress might determine. The inhabitants of the territory were not consulted; there was no provision that they should even be guaranteed a republican form of government like the States; they were secured no right of representation and given no vote. So, too, when it came to acquiring new territory, there was no thought of consulting the inhabitants. Mr. Jefferson did not ask the citizens of Louisiana to consent to their annexation, nor did Mr. Monroe submit such a question to the Spaniards of Florida, nor Mr. Polk to the Mexicans of California, nor Mr. Pierce to the New Mexicans, nor Mr. Johnson to the Russians and Aleuts of Alaska. The power of the Government to deal with territory, foreign or domestic, precisely as it chooses was understood from the beginning to be absolute; and at no stage in our whole history have we hesitated to exercise it. The question of permanently holding the Philippines or any other conquered territory as territory is not, and cannot be made, one of constitutional right; it is one solely of national duty and of national policy.

Does the Monroe Doctrine Interfere?

As a last resort, it is maintained that even if the Constitution does not forbid, the Monroe Doctrine does. But the famous declaration of Mr. Monroe on which reliance is placed does not warrant this conclusion. After holding that "the American continents, by the free and independent condition which they have assumed and maintained, are henceforth not to be considered as subjects for future colonization by any European Power," Mr. Monroe continued: "We should consider any attempt on their part to extend their system to any part of this hemisphere as dangerous to our peace and safety. With the existing colonies or dependencies of any European Power we have not interfered, and shall not interfere." The context makes it clear that this assurance applies solely to the existing colonies and dependencies they still had in this hemisphere; and that even this was qualified by the previous warning that while we took no part "in the wars of European Powers, in matters relating to themselves," we resented injuries and defended our rights. It will thus be seen that Mr. Monroe gave no pledge that we would never interfere with any dependency or colony of European Powers anywhere. He simply declared our general policy not to interfere with existing colonies still remaining to them on our coast, so long as they left the countries alone which had already gained their independence, and so long as they did not injure us or invade our rights. And even this statement of the scope of Mr. Monroe's declaration must be construed in the light of the fact that the same Administration which promulgated the Monroe Doctrine had already issued from the State Department Mr. Adams's prediction, above referred to, that "the annexation of Cuba will yet be found indispensable." Perhaps Mr. Monroe's language might have been properly understood as a general assurance that we would not meddle in Europe so long as they gave us no further trouble in America; but certainly it did not also abandon to their exclusive jurisdiction Asia and Africa and the islands of the sea.

The Necessary Outcome.

The candid conclusions seem inevitable that, not as a matter of policy, but as a necessity of the position in which we find ourselves and as a matter of national duty, we must hold Cuba, at least for a time and till a permanent government is well established for which we can afford to be responsible; we must hold Porto Rico; and we may have to hold the Philippines.

The war is a great sorrow, and to many these results of it will seem still more mournful. They cannot be contemplated with unmixed confidence by any; and to all who think, they must be a source of some grave apprehensions. Plainly, this unwelcome war is leading us by ways we have not trod to an end we cannot surely forecast. On the other hand, there are some good things coming from it that we can already see. It will make an end forever of Spain in this hemisphere. It will certainly secure to Cuba and Porto Rico better government. It will furnish an enormous outlet for the energy of our citizens, and give another example of the rapid development to which our system leads. It has already brought North and South together as nothing could but a foreign war in which both offered their blood for the cause of their reunited country—a result of incalculable advantage both at home and abroad. It has brought England and the United States together—another result of momentous importance in the progress of civilization and Christianity. Europe will know us better henceforth; even Spain will know us better; and this knowledge should tend powerfully hereafter to keep the peace of the world. The war should abate the swaggering, swash-buckler tendency of many of our public men, since it has shown our incredible unreadiness at the outset for meeting even a third-rate Power; and it must secure us henceforth an army and navy less ridiculously inadequate to our exposure. It insures us a mercantile marine. It insures the Nicaragua Canal, a Pacific cable, great development on our Pacific coast, and the mercantile control of the Pacific Ocean. It imposes new and very serious business on our public men, which ought to dignify and elevate the public service. Finally, it has shown such splendid courage and skill in the Army and Navy, such sympathy at home for our men at the front, and such devoted eagerness, especially among women, to alleviate suffering and humanize the struggle, as to thrill every patriotic heart and make us all prouder than ever of our country and its matchless people.

II

WAS IT TOO GOOD A TREATY?

This speech was made at a dinner given in New York by the Lotos Club in honor of Mr. Reid, who had been its president for fourteen years prior to his first diplomatic service abroad in 1889. It was the first public utterance by any one of the Peace Commissioners after the ratification of the Treaty of Paris.

Among the many letters of regret at the dinner, the following, from the Secretary of State and from his predecessor, were given to the public:

Washington, D.C., February 9, 1899.

To John Elderkin, Lotos Club, New York:

I received your note in due time, and had hoped until now to be able to come and join you in doing honor to my life-long friend, the Hon. Whitelaw Reid; but the pressure of official engagements here has made it impossible for me to do so. I shall be with you in spirit, and shall applaud to the best that can be said in praise of one who, in a life of remarkable variety of achievement, has honored every position he has held.

Faithfully yours,

John Hay.

Canton, Ohio, February 8, 1899.

To Chester S. Lord, Lotos Club, New York:

I beg to acknowledge the receipt of your invitation to attend the dinner to be given to the Hon. Whitelaw Reid on the evening of the 11th inst. Nothing would afford me more pleasure than to join the members of the Lotos Club in doing honor to Mr. Reid. It is a source of much regret that circumstances compel me to forego the privilege. His high character and worth, leadership in the best journalism of the day, eminent services, and wide experience long since gave him an honorable place among his contemporaries. The Commission to negotiate the treaty concluded at Paris on December 10 had no more valued member. His fellow-Commissioners were fortunate in being able to avail themselves of Mr. Reid's wide acquaintance with the leading statesmen and diplomats residing in Paris. His presence as a member of the Commission rendered unnecessary any further introduction to those who had known him as our Minister to France. He gave to the work of the Commission in unstinted measure the benefit of his wisdom in council, judgment, and skill in the preparation and presentation of the American case at Paris. Permit me to join you in congratulations and best wishes to Mr. Reid, and to express the hope that there are in store for him many more years of usefulness and honor.

Very truly yours,

William R. Day.

WAS IT TOO GOOD A TREATY?

Obviously the present occasion has no narrow or merely personal meaning. It comes to me only because I had the good fortune, through the friendly partiality of the President of the United States, to be associated with a great work in which you took a patriotic interest, and over the ratification of which you use this means of expressing your satisfaction. It was a happy thing for us to be able to bring back peace to our own land, and happier still to find that our treaty is accepted by the Senate and the people as one that guards the honor and protects the interests of the country. Only so should a nation like ours make peace at all.

Come, Peace, not like a mourner bowed

For honor lost and dear ones wasted,

But proud, to meet a people proud,

With eyes that tell of triumph tasted.

I shall make no apology—now that the Senate has unsealed our lips—for speaking briefly of this work just happily completed.

The only complaint one hears about it is that we did our duty too well—that, in fact, we made peace on terms too favorable to our own country. In all the pending discussion there seems to be no other fault found. On no other point is the treaty said by any one to be seriously defective.

It loyally carried out the attitude of Congress as to Cuba. It enforced the renunciation of Spanish sovereignty there, but, in spite of the most earnest Spanish efforts, it refused to accept American sovereignty. It loaded neither ourselves nor the Cubans with the so-called Cuban debts, incurred by Spain in the efforts to subdue them. It involved us in no complications, either in the West Indies or in the East, as to contracts or claims or religious establishments. It dealt liberally with a fallen foe—giving him a generous lump sum that more than covered any legitimate debts or expenditures for pacific improvements; assuming the burden of just claims against him by our own people; carrying back the armies surrendered on the other side of the world at our own cost; returning their arms; even restoring them their artillery, including heavy ordnance in field fortifications, munitions of war, and the very cattle that dragged their caissons. It secured alike for Cubans and Filipinos the release of political prisoners. It scrupulously reserved for Congress the power of determining the political status of the inhabitants of our new possessions. It declared on behalf of the most Protectionist country in the world for the policy of the Open Door within its Asiatic sphere of influence.

With all this the Senate and the country seemed content. But the treaty refused to return to Spanish rule one foot of territory over which that rule had been broken by the triumphs of our arms.

Were we to be reproached for that? Should the Senate have told us: "You overdid this business; you looked after the interests of your own country too thoroughly. You ought to have abandoned the great archipelago which the fortunes of war had placed at your country's disposal. You are not exactly unfaithful servants; you are too blindly, unswervingly faithful. You haven't seized an opportunity to run away from some distant results of the war into which Congress plunged the country before dreaming how far it might spread. You haven't dodged for us the responsibilities we incurred."

That is true. When Admiral Dewey sank the Spanish fleet, and General Merritt captured the Spanish army that alone maintained the Spanish hold on the Philippines, the Spanish power there was gone; and the civilization and the common sense and the Christianity of the world looked to the power that succeeded it to accept its responsibilities. So we took the Philippines. How could men representing this country, jealous of its honor, or with an adequate comprehension either of its duty or its rights, do otherwise?

A nation at war over a disputed boundary or some other material interest might properly stop when that interest was secured, and give back to the enemy all else that had been taken from him. But this was not a war for any material interest. It was a war to put down a rule over an alien people, which we declared so barbarous that we could no longer tolerate it. How could we consent to secure peace, after we had broken down this barbarous rule in two archipelagos, by agreeing that one of them should be forced back under it?

There was certainly another alternative. After destroying the only organized government in the archipelago, the only security for life and property, native and foreign, in great commercial centers like Manila, Iloilo, and Cebu, against hordes of uncivilized pagans and Mohammedan Malays, should we then scuttle out and leave them to their fate? A band of old-time Norse pirates, used to swooping down on a capital, capturing its rulers, seizing its treasure, burning the town, abandoning the people to domestic disorder and foreign spoliation, and promptly sailing off for another piratical foray—such a band of pirates might, no doubt, have left Manila to be sacked by the insurgents, while it fled from the Philippines. We did not think a self-respecting, civilized, responsible Christian Power could.

Indemnity.

There was another side to it. In a conflict to which fifty years of steadily increasing provocation had driven us we had lost 266 sailors on the *Maine*; had lost at Santiago and elsewhere uncounted victims of Spanish guns and tropical climates; and had spent in this war over $240,000,000, without counting the pensions that must still accrue under laws existing when it began. Where was the indemnity that, under such circumstances, it is the duty of the victorious nation to exact, not only in its own interest, but in the interest of a Christian civilization and the tendencies of modern International

Law, which require that a nation provoking unjust war shall smart for it, not merely while it lasts, but by paying the cost when it is ended? Spain had no money even to pay her own soldiers. No indemnity was possible, save in territory. Well, we once wanted to buy Cuba, before it had been desolated by twelve years of war and decimated by Weyler; yet our uttermost offer for it, our highest valuation even then, was $125,000,000—less than half the cost of our war. But now we were precluded from taking Cuba. Porto Rico, immeasurably less important to us, and eight hundred miles farther away from our coast, is only one twelfth the size of Cuba. Were the representatives of the United States, charged with the duty of protecting not only its honor, but its interests, in arranging terms of peace, to content themselves with little Porto Rico, away off a third of the way to Spain, plus the petty reef of Guam, in the middle of the Pacific, as indemnity for an unprovoked war that had cost and was to cost their country $300,000,000?

The Trouble they Give—are they Worth it?

But, some one exclaims, the Philippines are already giving us more trouble than they are worth! It is natural to say so just now, and it is partly true. What they are worth and likely to be worth to this country in the race for commercial supremacy on the Pacific—that is to say, for supremacy in the great development of trade in the Twentieth Century—is a question too large to be so summarily decided, or to be entered on at the close of a dinner, and under the irritation of a Malay half-breed's folly. But nobody ever doubted that they would give us trouble. That is the price nations must pay for going to war, even in a just cause. I was not one of those who were eager to begin this war with Spain; but I protest against any attempt to evade our just responsibility in the position in which it has left us. We shall have trouble in the Philippines. So we shall have trouble in Cuba and in Porto Rico. If we dawdle, and hesitate, and lead them to think we fear them and fear trouble, our trouble will be great. If, on the other hand, we grasp this nettle danger, if we act promptly, with inexorable vigor and with justice, it may be slight. At any rate, the more serious the crisis the plainer our path. God give us the courage to purify our politics and strengthen our Government to meet these new and grave duties!

III

PURPORT OF THE TREATY

This speech was made, two days after the preceding one, on the invitation of the Marquette Club of Chicago, at the dinner of six hundred which it gave in the Auditorium Hotel, February 13, 1899, in honor of Lincoln's birthday.

PURPORT OF THE TREATY

Beyond the Alleghanies the American voice rings clear and true. It does not sound, here in Chicago, as if you favored the pursuit of partizan aims in great questions of foreign policy, or division among our own people in the face of insurgent guns turned upon our soldiers on the distant fields to which we sent them. We are all here, it would seem, to stand by the peace that has been secured, even if we have to fight for it.

Neither has any reproach come from Chicago to the Peace Commissioners because, when intrusted with your interests in a great negotiation in a foreign capital, they made a settlement on terms too favorable to their own country—because in bringing home peace with honor they also brought home more property than some of our people wanted! When that reproach has been urged elsewhere, it has recalled the familiar defense against a similar complaint in an old political contest. There might, it was said, be some serious disadvantages about a surplus in the national Treasury; but, at any rate, it was easier to deal with a surplus than with a deficit! If we have brought back too much, that is only a question for Congress and our voters. If we had brought back too little, it might have been again a question for the Army and the Navy.

No one of you has ever been heard to find fault with an agent because in making a difficult settlement he got all you wanted, and a free option on something further that everybody else wanted! Do you know of any other civilized nation of the first or even of the second class that wouldn't jump at that option on the Philippines? Ask Russia. Ask Germany. Ask Japan. Ask England or France. Ask little Belgium![1] And yet, what one of them, unless it be Japan, has any conceivable interest in the Philippines to be compared with that of the mighty Republic which now commands the one side of the

Pacific, and, unless this American generation is blinder to opportunity than any of its predecessors, will soon command the other?

Put yourselves for a moment in our place on the Quai d'Orsay. Would you really have had your representatives in Paris, the guardians of your honor in negotiating peace with your enemy, declare that while Spanish rule in the West Indies was so barbarous that it was our duty to destroy it, we were now so eager for peace that for its sake we were willing in the East to reëstablish that same barbarous rule? Or would you have had your agents in Paris, the guardians also of your material interests, throw away all chance for indemnity for a war that began with the loss of 266 American sailors on the *Maine*, and had cost your Treasury during the year over $240,000,000? Would you have had them throw away a magnificent foothold for the trade of the farther East, which the fortune of war had placed in your hand, throw away a whole archipelago of boundless possibilities, economic and strategic, throw away the opportunity of centuries for your country? Would you have had them, on their own responsibility, then and there decide this question for all time, and absolutely refuse to reserve it for the decision of Congress and of the American people, to whom that decision belongs, and who have the right to an opportunity first for its deliberate consideration?

Some Features in the Treaty.

Your toast is to the "Achievements of American Diplomacy." Not such were its achievements under your earlier statesmen; not such has been its work under the instructions of your State Department, from John Quincy Adams on down the honored line; and not such the work your representatives brought back to you from Paris.

They were dealing with a nation with whom it has never been easy to make peace, even when war was no longer possible; but they secured a peace treaty without a word that compromises the honor or endangers the interests of the country.

They scrupulously reserved for your own decision, through your Congress or at the polls, the question of political status and civil rights for the inhabitants of your new possessions.

They resisted adroit Spanish efforts for special privileges and guaranties for their established church, and pledged the United States to absolute freedom in the exercise of their religion for all these recent Spanish subjects—pagan, Mohammedan, Confucian, or Christian.

They maintained, in the face of the most vehement opposition, not merely of Spain, but of well-nigh all Europe, a principle vital to oppressed people struggling for freedom—a principle without which our own freedom could not have been established, and without which any successful revolt against any unjust rule could be made practically impossible. That principle is that, contrary to the prevailing rule and practice in large transfers of sovereignty, debts do not necessarily follow the territory if incurred by the mother country distinctly in efforts to enslave it. Where so incurred, your representatives persistently and successfully maintained that no attempt by the mother country to mortgage to bondholders the revenues of custom-houses or in any way to pledge the future income of the territory could be recognized as a valid or binding security—that the moment the hand of the oppressor relaxed its grasp, his claim on the future revenues of the oppressed territory was gone. It is a doctrine that raised an outcry in every Continental bourse, and struck terror to every gambling European investor in national loans, floated at usurious profits, to raise funds for unjust wars. But it is right, and one may be proud that the United States stood like a rock, barring any road to peace which led to loading either on the liberated territory or on the people that had freed it the debts incurred in the wars against it. If this is not International Law now, it will be; and the United States will have made it.

But your representatives in Paris placed your country in no tricky attitude of endeavoring either to evade or repudiate just obligations. They recognized the duty of reimbursement for debts legitimately incurred for pacific improvements or otherwise, for the real benefit of the transferred territory. Not till it began to appear that, of the Philippine debt of forty millions Mexican, or a little under twenty millions of our money, a fourth had been transferred direct to aid the war in Cuba, and the rest had probably been spent mainly in the war in Luzon, did your representatives hesitate at its payment; and even then they decided to give a lump sum equal to it, which could serve as a recognition of whatever debts Spain might have incurred in the past for expenditures in that archipelago for the benefit of the people.

They protected what was gained in the war from adroit efforts to put it all at risk again, through an untimely appeal to the noble principle of Arbitration. They held—and I am sure the best friends of the principle will thank them for holding—that an honest resort to Arbitration must come before war, to avert its horrors, not after war, to escape its consequences.

They were enabled to pledge the most Protectionist country in the world to the liberal and wise policy of the Open Door in the East.

And finally they secured that diplomatic novelty, a treaty in which the acutest senatorial critics have not found a peg on which inadmissible claims against the country may be hung.

The Material Side of the Business.

At the same time they neither neglected nor feared the duty of caring for the material interests of their own country;—the duty of grasping the enormous possibilities upon which we had stumbled, for sharing in the awakening and development of the farther East. That way lies now the best hope of American commerce. There you may command a natural rather than an artificial trade—a trade which pushes itself instead of needing to be pushed; a trade with people who can send you things you want and cannot produce, and take from you in return things they want and cannot produce; in other words, a trade largely between different zones, and largely with less advanced peoples, comprising nearly one fourth the population of the globe, whose wants promise to be speedily and enormously developed.

The Atlantic Ocean carries mainly a different trade, with people as advanced as ourselves, who could produce or procure elsewhere much of what they buy from us, while we could produce, if driven to it, most of what we need to buy from them. It is more or less, therefore, an artificial trade, as well as a trade in which we have lost the first place and will find it difficult to regain. The ocean carriage for the Atlantic is in the hands of our rivals.

The Pacific Ocean, on the contrary, is in our hands now. Practically we own more than half the coast on this side, dominate the rest, and have midway stations in the Sandwich and Aleutian Islands. To extend now the authority of the United States over the great Philippine Archipelago is to fence in the China Sea and secure an almost equally commanding position on the other side of the Pacific—doubling our control of it and of the fabulous trade the Twentieth Century will see it bear. Rightly used, it enables the United States to convert the Pacific Ocean almost into an American lake.

Are we to lose all this through a mushy sentimentality, characteristic neither of practical nor of responsible people—alike un-American and un-Christian, since it would humiliate us by showing lack of nerve to hold what we are entitled to, and incriminate us by entailing endless bloodshed and anarchy on a people whom we have already stripped of the only government they have known for three hundred years, and whom we should thus abandon to civil war and foreign spoliation?

Bugbears.

Let us free our minds of some bugbears. One of them is this notion that with the retention of the Philippines our manufacturers will be crushed by the products of cheap Eastern labor. But it does not abolish our custom-houses, and we can still enforce whatever protection we desire.

Another is that our American workmen will be swamped under the immigration of cheap Eastern labor. But tropical laborers rarely emigrate to colder climates. Few have ever come. If we need a law to keep them out, we can make it.

It is a bugbear that the Filipinos would be citizens of the United States, and would therefore have the same rights of free travel and free entry of their own manufactures with other citizens. The treaty did not make them citizens of the United States at all; and they never will be, unless you neglect your Congress.

It is a bugbear that anybody living on territory or other property belonging to the United States must be a citizen. The Constitution says that "persons born or naturalized in the United States are citizens of the United States"; while it adds in the same sentence, "and of the State wherein they reside," showing plainly that the provision was not then meant to include territories.

It is equally a bugbear that the tariff must necessarily be the same over any of the territory or other property of the United States as it is in the Nation itself. The Constitution requires that "all duties, imposts, and excises shall be the same throughout the United States," and while there was an incidental expression from the Supreme Bench in 1820 to the effect that the name United States as here used should include the District of Columbia and other territory, it was no part even then of the decision actually rendered, and it would be absurd to stretch this mere dictum of three quarters of a century ago, relating then, at any rate, to this continent alone, to carry the Dingley tariff now across to the antipodes.

Duties of the Hour.

Brushing aside, then, these bugbears, gentlemen, what are the obvious duties of the hour?

First, hold what you are entitled to. If you are ever to part with it, wait at least till you have examined it and found out that you have no use for it. Before yielding to temporary difficulties at the outset, take time to be quite sure you are ready now to abandon your chance for a commanding position in the trade of China, in the commercial control of the Pacific Ocean, and in the richest commercial development of the approaching century.

Next, resist admission of any of our new possessions as States, or their organization on a plan designed to prepare them for admission. Stand firm for the present American Union of sister States, undiluted by anybody's archipelagos.

Make this fight easiest by making it at the beginning. Resist the first insidious effort to change the character of this Union by leaving the continent. The danger commences with the first extra-continental State. We want no Porto Ricans or Cubans to be sending Senators and Representatives to Washington to help govern the American Continent, any more than we want Kanakas or Tagals or Visayans or Mohammedan Malays. We will do them good and not harm, if we may, all the days of our life; but, please God, we will not divide this Republic, the heritage of our fathers, among them.

Resist the crazy extension of the doctrine that government derives its just powers from the consent of the governed to an extreme never imagined by the men who framed it, and never for one moment acted upon in their own practice. Why should we force Jefferson's language to a meaning Jefferson himself never gave it in dealing with the people of Louisiana, or Andrew Jackson in dealing with those of South Carolina, or Abraham Lincoln with the seceding States, or any responsible statesman of the country at any period in its history in dealing with Indians or New Mexicans or Californians or Russians? What have the Tagals done for us that we should treat them better and put them on a plane higher than any of these?

And next, resist alike either schemes for purely military governments, or schemes for territorial civil governments, with offices to be filled up, according to the old custom, by "carpet-baggers" from the United States, on an allotment of increased patronage, fairly divided among the "bosses" of the different States. Egypt under Lord Cromer is an object-lesson of what may be done in a more excellent way by men of our race in dealing with such a problem. Better still, and right under our eyes, is the successful solution of the identical problem that confronts us, in the English organization and administration of the federated Malay States on the Malacca Peninsula.

The Opposition as Old as Webster.

I wish to speak with respect of the sincere and conscientious opposition to all these conclusions, manifest chiefly in the East and in the Senate; and with especial respect of the eminent statesman who has headed that opposition. No man will question his ability, his moral elevation, or the courage with which he follows his intellectual and moral convictions. But I may be permitted to remind you that the noble State he worthily represents is not now counted for the first time against the interest and the development of the country. In February, 1848, Daniel Webster, speaking for the same great State and in the same high forum, conjured up precisely the same visions of the destruction of the Constitution, and proclaimed the same hostility to new territory. Pardon me while I read you half a dozen sentences, and note how curiously they sound like an echo—

or a prophecy—of what we have lately been hearing from the Senate:

> Will you take peace without territory and preserve the integrity of the Constitution of the country?... I think I see a course adopted which is likely to turn the Constitution of this land into a deformed monster—into a curse rather than a blessing.... There would not be two hundred families of persons who would emigrate from the United States to New Mexico for agricultural purposes in fifty years.... I have never heard of anything, and I cannot conceive of anything, more absurd and more affrontive of all sober judgment than the cry that we are getting indemnity by the acquisition of New Mexico and California. I hold that they are not worth a dollar!

It was merely that splendid empire in itself, stretching from Los Angeles and San Francisco eastward to Denver, that was thus despised and rejected of Massachusetts. And it was only fifty years ago! With all due respect, a great spokesman of Massachusetts is as liable to mistake in this generation as in the last.

Lack of Faith in the People.

It is fair, I think, to say that this whole hesitation over the treaty of peace is absolutely due to lack of faith in our own people, distrust of the methods of administration they may employ in the government of distant possessions, and distrust of their ability to resist the schemes of demagogues for promoting the ultimate admission of Kanaka and Malay and half-breed commonwealths to help govern the continental Republic of our pride, this homogeneous American Union of sovereign States. If there is real reason to fear that the American people cannot restrain themselves from throwing open the doors of their Senate and House of Representatives to such sister States as Luzon, or the Visayas, or the Sandwich Islands, or Porto Rico, or even Cuba, then the sooner we beg some civilized nation, with more common sense and less sentimentality and gush, to take them off our hands the better. If we are unequal to a manly and intelligent discharge of the responsibilities the war has entailed, then let us confess our unworthiness, and beg Japan to assume the duties of a civilized Christian state toward the Philippines, while England can extend the same relief to us in Cuba and Porto Rico. But having thus ignominiously shirked the position demanded by our belligerency and our success, let us never again presume to take a place among the self-respecting and responsible nations of the earth that can ever lay us liable to another such task. If called to it, let us at the outset admit our unfitness, withdraw within our own borders, and leave these larger duties of the world to less incapable races or less craven rulers.

Far other and brighter are the hopes I have ventured to cherish concerning the course of the American people in this emergency. I have thought there was encouragement for nations as well as for individuals in remembering the sobering and steadying influence of great responsibilities suddenly devolved. When Prince Hal comes to the crown he is apt to abjure Falstaff. When we come to the critical and dangerous work of controlling turbulent semi-tropical dependencies, the agents we choose cannot be the ward heelers of the local bosses. Now, if ever, is the time to rally the brain and conscience of the American people to a real elevation and purification of their Civil Service, to the most exalted standards of public duty, to the most strenuous and united effort of all men of good will to make our Government worthy of the new and great responsibilities which the Providence of God rather than any purpose of man has imposed upon it.

IV

THE DUTIES OF PEACE

A speech made at the dinner given by the Ohio Society in honor of the Peace Commissioners, in the Waldorf-Astoria Hotel, New York, February 25, 1899.

THE DUTIES OF PEACE

You call and I obey. Any call from Ohio, wherever it finds me, is at once a distinction and a duty. But it would be easier to-night and more natural for me to remain silent. I am one of yourselves, the givers of the feast, and the occasion belongs peculiarly to my colleagues on the Peace Commission. I regret that more of them are not here to tell you in person how profoundly we all appreciate the compliment you pay us. Judge Day, after an experience and strain the like of which few Americans of this generation have so suddenly and so successfully met, is seeking to regain his strength at the South; Senator Frye, at the close of an anxious session, finds his responsible duties in Washington too exacting to permit even a day's absence; and Senator Davis, who could not leave the care of the treaty to visit his State even when his own reëlection was pending, has at last snatched the first moment of relief since he was sent to Paris last summer, to go out to St. Paul and meet the constituents who have in his absence renewed to him the crown of a good and faithful servant.

It is all the more fortunate, therefore, that you are honored by the presence of the patriotic member of the opposition who formed the regulator and balance-wheel of the Commission. When Senator Gray objected, we all reëxamined the processes of our reasoning. When he assented, we knew at once we must be on solid ground and went ahead. It was an expected gratification to have with you also the accomplished secretary and counsel to the Commission, a man as modest and unobtrusive as its president, and, like him, equal to any summons. In his regretted absence, we rejoice to find here the most distinguished military aid ordered to report to the Commission, and the most important witness before it—the Conqueror of Manila.

So much you will permit me to say in my capacity as one of the hosts, rather than as a member of the body to which you pay this gracious compliment.

It is not for me to speak of another figure necessarily missing tonight, though often with you heretofore at these meetings—the member of the Ohio Society who sent us to Paris! A great and shining record already speaks for him. He will be known in our history as the President who freed America from the last trace of Spanish blight; who realized the aspiration of our earlier statesmen, cherished by the leaders of either party through three quarters of a century, for planting the flag both on Cuba and on the Sandwich Islands; more than this, as the President who has carried that flag half-way round the world and opened the road for the trade of the Nation to follow it.

All this came from simply doing his duty from day to day, as that duty was forced upon him. No other man in the United States held back from war as he did, risking loss of popularity, risking the hostility of Congress, risking the harsh judgment of friends in agonizing for peace. It was no doubt in the spirit of the Prince of Peace, but it was also with the wisdom of Polonius: "Beware of entrance to a quarrel; but, being in, bear it, that the opposer may beware of thee!" Never again will any nation imagine that it can trespass indefinitely against the United States with impunity. Never again will an American war-ship run greater risks in a peaceful harbor than in battle. The world will never again be in doubt whether, when driven to war, we will end it in a gush of sentimentality or a shiver of unmanly apprehension over untried responsibilities, by fleeing from our plain duty, and hastening to give up what we are entitled to, before we have even taken an opportunity to look at it.

Does Peace Pacify?

But it must be confessed that "looking at it" during the past week has not been an altogether cheerful occupation. While the aspect of some of these new possessions remains so frowning there are faint hearts ready enough to say that the Peace Commission is in no position to be receiving compliments. Does protection protect? is an old question that used to be thrown in our faces—though I believe even the questioners finally made up their minds that it did. Does peace pacify? is the question of the hour. Well, as to our original antagonist, historic, courageous Spain, there seems ground to hope and believe and be glad that it does—not merely toward us, but within her own borders. When she jettisoned cargo that had already shifted ruinously, there is reason to think that she averted disaster and saved the ship. Then, as to Porto Rico there is no doubt of peace; and as to Cuba very little—although it would be too much to hope that her twelve years of civil war could be followed by an absolute calm, without disorders.

As to other possessions in the farther East, we may as well recognize at once that we are dealing now with the same sort of clever barbarians as in the earlier days of the Republic, when, on another ocean not then less distant, we were compelled to encounter the Algerine pirates. But there is this difference. Then we merely chastised the Algerines into letting us and our commerce alone. The permanent policing of that coast of the Mediterranean was not imposed upon us by surrounding circumstances, or by any act of ours; it belonged to nearer nations. Now a war we made has broken down the only authority that existed to protect the commerce of the world in one of its greatest Eastern thoroughfares, and to preserve the lives and property of people of all nations resorting to those marts. We broke it down, and we cannot, dare not, display the cowardice and selfishness of failing to replace it. However men may differ as to our future policy in those regions, there can be no difference as to our present duty. It is as plain as that of putting down a riot in Chicago or New York—all the plainer because, until recently, we have ourselves been taking the very course and doing the very things to encourage the rioters.

Why Take Sovereignty?

A distinguished and patriotic citizen said to me the other day, in a Western city: "You might have avoided this trouble in the Senate by refusing title in the Philippines exactly as in Cuba, and simply enforcing renunciation of Spanish sovereignty. Why didn't you do it?" The question is important, and the reason ought to be understood. But at the outset it should be clearly realized that the circumstances which made it possible to take that course as to Cuba were altogether exceptional. For three quarters of a century we had asserted a special interest and right of interference there as against any other nation. The island is directly on our coast, and no one doubted that at least as much order as in the past would be preserved there, even if we had to do it ourselves. There was also the positive action of Congress, which, on the one hand, gave us excuse for refusing a sovereignty our highest legislative authority had disclaimed, and, on the other, formally cast the shield of our responsibility over Cuba when left without a government or a sovereignty. Besides, there was a people there, advanced enough, sufficiently compact and homogeneous in religion, race, and language, sufficiently used already to the methods of government, to warrant our republican claim that the sovereignty was not being left in the air—that it was only left where, in the last analysis, in a civilized community, it must always reside, in the people themselves.

And yet, under all these conditions, the most difficult task your Peace Commissioners had at Paris was to maintain and defend the demand for a renunciation of sovereignty without anybody's acceptance of the sovereignty thus renounced. International Law has not been so understood abroad; and it may be frankly confessed that the Spanish arguments were learned, acute, sustained by the general judgment of Europe, and not easy to refute.

A similar demand concerning the Philippines neither could nor ought to have been acquiesced in by the civilized world. Here were ten millions of people on a great highway of commerce, of numerous different races, different languages, different religions, some semi-civilized, some barbarous, others mere pagan savages, but without a majority or even a respectable minority of them accustomed to self-government or believed to be capable of it. Sovereignty over such a conglomeration and in such a place could not be left in the air. The civilized world would not recognize its transfer, unless transferred to somebody. Renunciation under such circumstances would have been equivalent in International Law to abandonment, and that would have been equivalent to anarchy and a race for seizure among the nations that could get there quickest.

We could, of course, have refused to accept the obligations of a civilized, responsible nation. After breaking down government in those commercial centers, we could have refused to set up anything in its stead, and simply washed our hands of the whole business; but to do that would have been to show ourselves more insensible to moral obligations than if we had restored them outright to Spain.

How to Deal with the Philippines.

Well, if the elephant must be on our hands, what are we going to do with it? I venture to answer that first we must put down the riot. The lives and property of German and British merchants must be at least as safe in Manila as they were under Spanish rule before we are ready for any other step whatever.

Next, ought we not to try to diagnose our case before we turn every quack doctor among us loose on it—understand what the problem is before beginning heated partizan discussions as to the easiest way of solving it? And next, shall we not probably fare best in the end if we try to profit somewhat by the experience others have had in like cases?

The widest experience has been had by the great nation whose people and institutions are nearest like our own. Illustrations of her successful methods may be found in Egypt and in many British dependencies, but, for our purposes, probably best of all either on the Malay Peninsula or on the north coast of Borneo, where she has had the happiest results in dealing with intractable types of the worst of these same races. Some rules drawn from this experience might be distasteful to people who look upon new possessions as merely so much more government patronage, and quite repugnant to the noble army of office-seekers; but they surely mark the path of safety.

The first is to meddle at the outset as little as possible with every native custom and institution and even prejudice; the next is to use every existing native agency you can; and the next to employ in the government service just as few Americans as you can, and only of the best. Convince the natives of your irresistible power and your inexorable purpose, then of your desire to be absolutely just, and after that—not before—be as kind as you can. At the outset you will doubtless find your best agents among the trained officers of the Navy and the Army, particularly the former. On the retired list of both, but again particularly of the Navy, ought to be found just the experience in contact with foreign races, the moderation, wide views, justice, rigid method, and inflexible integrity, you need. Later on should come a real civil service, with such pure and efficient administration abroad as might help us ultimately to conclude that we ourselves deserve as well as the heathen, and induce us to set up similar standards for our own service at home. Meantime, if we have taught the heathen largely to govern themselves without being a hindrance and menace to the civilization and the commerce of the world, so much the better. Heaven speed the day! If not, we must even continue to be responsible for them ourselves—a duty we did not seek, but should be ashamed to shirk.

V

THE OPEN DOOR

A speech made at the dinner given by the American-Asiatic Association in honor of Rear-Admiral Lord Charles Beresford, at Delmonico's, New York, February 23, 1899.

THE OPEN DOOR

The hour is late, you have already enjoyed your intellectual feast, you have heard the man you came to hear, and I shall detain you for but a moment. The guest whom we are all here to honor and applaud is returning from a journey designed to promote the safety and extension of his country's trade in the Chinese Orient. He has probably been accustomed to think of us as the most extreme Protectionist nation in the world; and he may have heard at first of our recent acquisition on the China Sea with some apprehension on that very account.

United States a Free-Trade Country.

Now, there are two facts that might be somewhat suggestive to any who take that view. One is that, though we may be "enraged Protectionists," as our French friends occasionally call us, we have rarely sought to extend the protective system where we had nothing and could develop nothing to protect. The other is that we are also the greatest free-trade country in the world. Nowhere else on the globe does absolute free trade prevail over so wide, rich, and continuous an expanse of territory, with such variety and volume of production and manufacture; and nowhere have its beneficent results been more conspicuous. From the Golden Gate your guest has crossed a continent teeming with population and manufactures without encountering a custom-house. If he had come back from China the other way, from Suez to London, he would have passed a dozen!

When your Peace Commissioners were brought face to face with the retention of the Philippines, they were at liberty to consider the question it raised for immediate action in the light of both sides of the national practice. Here was an archipelago practically without manufactures to protect, or need for protection to develop manufactures; and here were swarming populations with whom trade was sure to increase and ramify, in proportion to its freedom from obstructions. Thus it came about that your Commissioners were led to a view which to many has seemed a new departure, and were finally enabled to preface an offer to Spain with the remark that it was the policy of the United States to maintain in the Philippines an open door to the world's commerce. Great Protectionist leader as the President is and long has been, he sanctioned the declaration; and Protectionist as is the Senate, it ratified the pledge.

The Open Door.

Under treaty guaranty Spain is now entitled to the Open Door in the Philippines for ten years. Under the most favored nation clause, what is thus secured to Spain would not be easily refused, even if any one desired it, to any other nation; and the door that stands open there for the next ten years will by that time have such a rising tide of trade pouring through it from the awakening East that no man thenceforward can ever close it.

There are two ways of dealing with the trade of a distant dependency. You may give such advantage to your own people as practically to exclude everybody else. That was the Spanish way. That is the French way. Neither nation has grown rich of late on its colonial extensions. Again, you may impose such import or export duties as will raise the revenue needed for the government of the territory, to be paid by all comers at its ports on a basis of absolute equality. In some places that is the British way. Henceforth, in the Philippines, that is the United States way. The Dingley tariff is not to be transferred to the antipodes.

Protectionists or Free-traders, I believe we may all rejoice in this as best for the Philippines and best for ourselves. I venture to think that we may rejoice over it, too, with your distinguished guest. It enables Great Britain and the United States to preserve a common interest and present a common front in the enormous commercial development in the East that must attend the awakening of the Chinese Colossus; and whenever and wherever Great Britain and the United States stand together, the peace and the civilization of the world will be the better for it.

VI

SOME CONSEQUENCES OF THE TREATY OF PARIS

This discussion of the advances in International Law and changes in national policy traceable to the negotiations that ended in the Peace of Paris, was written in March, for the first number of "The Anglo-Saxon Review" (then announced for May), which appeared in June, 1899.

SOME CONSEQUENCES OF THE TREATY OF PARIS

In 1823 Thomas Jefferson, writing from the retirement of Monticello to James Monroe, then President of the United States, said:

Great Britain is the nation which can do us the most harm of any one on all the earth, and with her on our side we need not fear the world. With her, then, we should most sedulously cherish a cordial friendship, and nothing would tend more to knit our affections than to be fighting once more, side by side, in the same cause.

As these lines are written,[2] the thing which Jefferson looked forward to has, in a small way, come to pass. For the first time under government orders since British regulars and the militia of the American colonies fought Indians on Lake Champlain and the French in Canada, the Briton and the American have been fighting side by side, and again against savages. In a larger sense, too, they are at last embarked side by side in the Eastern duty, devolved on each, of "bearing the white man's burden." It seems natural, now, to count on such a friendly British interest in present American problems as may make welcome a brief statement of some things that were settled by the late Peace of Paris, and some that were unsettled.

Whether treaties really settle International Law is itself an unsettled point. English and American writers incline to give them less weight in that regard than is the habit of the great Continental authorities. But it is reasonable to think that some of the points insisted upon by the United States in the Treaty of Paris will be precedents as weighty, henceforth, in international policy as they are now novel to international practice. If not International Law yet, they probably will be; and it is confidently assumed that they will command the concurrence of the British government and people, as well as of the most intelligent and dispassionate judgment on the Continent.

When Arbitration is Inadmissible.

The distinct and prompt refusal by the American Commissioners to submit questions at issue between them and their Spanish colleagues to arbitration marks a limit to the application of that principle in international controversy which even its friends will be apt hereafter to welcome. No civilized nation is more thoroughly committed to the policy of international arbitration than the United States. The Spanish Commissioners were able to reinforce their appeal for it by striking citations from the American record: the declaration of the Senate of Massachusetts, as early as 1835, in favor of an international court for the peaceful settlement of all disputes between nations; the action of the Senate of the United States in 1853, favoring a clause in all future treaties with foreign countries whereby difficulties that could not be settled by diplomacy should be referred to arbitrators; the concurrence of the two Houses, twenty years later, in reaffirming this principle; and at last their joint resolution, in 1888, requesting the President to secure agreements to that end with all nations with whom he maintained diplomatic intercourse.

But the American Commissioners at once made it clear that the rational place for arbitration is as a substitute for war, not as a second remedy, to which the contestant may still have a right to resort after having exhausted the first. In the absence of the desired obligation to arbitrate, the dissatisfied nation, according to the American theory, may have, after diplomacy has completely failed, a choice of remedies, but not a double remedy. It may choose arbitration, or it may choose war; but the American Commissioners flatly refused to let it choose war, and then, after defeat, claim still the right to call in arbitrators and put again at risk before them the verdict of war. Arbitration comes before war, they insisted, to avert its horrors; not after war, to afford the defeated party a chance yet to escape its consequences.

The principle thus stated is thought self-evidently sound and just. Americans were surprised to find how completely it was overlooked in the contemporaneous European discussion—how general was the sympathy with the Spanish request for arbitration, and how naïf the apparently genuine surprise at the instant and unqualified refusal to consider it. Even English voices joined in the chorus of encouraging approval that, from every quarter in Europe, greeted the formal Spanish appeal for an opportunity to try over in another forum the questions they had already submitted to the arbitrament of arms. The more clearly the American view is now recognized and accepted, the greater must be the tendency in the future to seek arbitration at the outset. To refuse arbitration when only sought at the end of war, and as a means of escaping its consequences, is certainly to stimulate efforts for averting war at the beginning of difficulties by means of arbitration. The refusal prevents such degradation of a noble reform to an ignoble end as would make arbitration the refuge, not of those who wish to avoid war, but only of those who have preferred war and been beaten at it. The American precedent should thus become a powerful influence for promoting the cause of genuine international arbitration, and so for the preservation of peace between nations.

Does Debt Follow Sovereignty?

Equally unexpected and important to the development of ordered liberty and good government in the world was the American refusal to accept any responsibility, for themselves or for the Cubans, on account of the so-called Cuban debt. The principle asserted from the outset by the American Commissioners, and finally maintained, in negotiating the Peace of Paris, was that a national debt incurred in efforts to subdue a colony, even if called a colonial debt, or secured by a pledge of colonial revenues, cannot be attached in the nature of a mortgage to the territory of that colony, so that when the colony gains its independence it may still be held for the cost of the unsuccessful efforts to keep it in subjection.

The first intimations that no part of the so-called Cuban debt would either be assumed by the United States or transferred with the territory to the Cubans, were met with an outcry from every bourse in Europe. Bankers, investors, and the financial world in general had taken it for granted that bonds which had been regularly issued by the Power exercising sovereignty over the territory, and which specifically pledged the revenues of custom-houses in that territory for the payment of the interest and ultimately of the principal, must be recognized. Not to do it, they said, would be bald, unblushing repudiation—a thing least to be looked for or tolerated in a nation of spotless credit and great wealth, which in past times of trial had made many sacrifices to preserve its financial honor untarnished.

It must be admitted that modern precedents were not altogether in favor of the American position. Treaties ceding territory not infrequently provide for the assumption by the new sovereign of a proportional part of the general obligations of the ceding state. This is usually true when the territory ceded is so considerable as to form an important portion of the dismembered country. Even "the great conqueror of this century," as the Spanish Commissioners exclaimed in one of their arguments, "never dared to violate this rule of eternal justice in any of the treaties he concluded with those sovereigns whose territories he appropriated, in whole or in part, as a reward for his victories." They cited his first treaty of August 24, 1801, with Bavaria providing that the debts of the duchy of Deux-Ponts, and of that part of the Palatinate acquired by France, should follow the countries, and challenged the production of any treaty of Napoleon's or of any modern treaty where the principle of such transfer was violated.

They were able to base a stronger claim on the precedents of the New World. They were, indeed, betrayed into some curious errors. One was that the thirteen original States, at the close of the Revolutionary War, paid over to Great Britain fifteen million pounds as their share of the public debt. Another was that the payment of the Texas debt by the United States must be a precedent now for its payment of the Cuban debt—whereas the Texas debt was incurred by the Texas insurgents in their successful war for independence, while the Cuban debt was incurred by the mother country in her unsuccessful effort to put down the Cuban insurgents. But as to the Spanish-American republics, they were more nearly on solid ground. It was true, and was more to the point than most of their other citations, that every one of these Spanish-American republics assumed its debt, that most of them did it before their independence was recognized, and that they gave these debts contracted by Spain the preference over later debts contracted by themselves. The language in the treaty with Bolivia was particularly sweeping. It assumed as its own these debts of every kind whatsoever, "including all incurred for pensions, salaries, supplies, advances, transportation, forced loans, deposits, contracts, and any other debts incurred during war-times or prior thereto, chargeable to said treasuries; provided they were contracted by direct orders of the Spanish government or its constituted authorities in said territories." The Argentine Republic and Uruguay, in negotiating their treaties, expressed the same idea more tersely: "Just as it acquires the rights and privileges belonging to the crown of Spain, so it also assumes all the duties and obligations of the crown."

The argument was certainly obvious, and at first sight seemed fair, that what every other revolted American colony of Spain had done, on gaining its independence, the last of the long line should also do. But an examination shows that in no case were the circumstances such as to make it a fair precedent for Cuba. In the other colonies the debts were largely due to their own people. To a considerable extent they had been incurred for the prosecution of improvements of a pacific character, generally for the public good and often at the public desire. Another part had been spent in the legitimate work of preserving public order and extending the advantages of government over wild regions and native tribes.[3] The rich, compact, populous island of Cuba had called for no such loans up to the time when Spain had already lost all of her American colonies on the continent, and had consequently no other dependency on which to fasten her exacting governor-generals and hosts of other official leeches. There was no Cuban debt. Any honest administration had ample revenues for all legitimate expenses, and a surplus; and this surplus seems not to have been used for the benefit of the island, but sent home. Between 1856 and 1861 over $20,000,000 of Cuban surplus were thus remitted to Madrid. Next began a plan for using Cuban credit as a means of raising money to re-conquer the lost dominions; and so "Cuban bonds" (with the guaranty of the Spanish nation) were issued, first for the effort to regain Santo Domingo, and then for the expedition to Mexico. By 1864 $3,000,000 had been so issued; by 1868 $18,000,000—not at the request or with the consent of the Cubans, and not for their benefit. Then commenced the Cuban insurrection; and from that time on, all Spain could wring from Cuba or borrow in European markets on the pledge of Cuban revenues and her own guaranty went in the effort to subdue a colony in revolt against her injustice and bad government. The lenders knew the facts and took the risk. Two years after this first insurrection was temporarily put down, these so-called Cuban debts had amounted to over $170,000,000. They were subsequently consolidated into other and later issues; but whatever change of form or date they underwent, they continued to represent practically just three things: the effort to conquer Santo Domingo, the expedition to Mexico, and the efforts to subdue Cuba. A movement to refund at a lower rate of interest was begun in 1890, and for this purpose an issue of $175,000,000 of Spanish bonds was authorized, to be paid out of the revenues of Cuba, but with the guaranty of the Spanish nation. Before many had been placed the insurrection had again broken out. Thenceforward they were used not to refund old bonds, but to raise money for the prosecution of the new war. Before its close this indebtedness had been swollen to over double the figure named above, and a part of the money must have been used directly in the war against the United States.

In the negotiations Spain took high moral ground with reference to these debts. She utterly denied any right to inquire how the proceeds had been expended. She did not insist for her own benefit on their recognition and transfer with the territory. She was concerned, not for herself, but for international morality and for the innocent holders. Some, no doubt, were Spanish citizens, but many others were French, or Austrian, or of other foreign nationalities. The bonds were freely dealt in on the Continental bourses. A failure to provide for them would be a public scandal throughout civilization; it would cause a wide-spread and profound shock to the sense of security in national obligations the world over, besides incalculable injustice and individual distress.

But the fact was that these were the bonds of the Spanish nation, issued by the Spanish nation for its own purposes, guaranteed in terms "by the faith of the Spanish nation," and with another guaranty pledging Spanish sovereignty and control over certain colonial revenues. Spain failed to maintain her title to the security she had pledged, but the lenders knew the instability of that security when they risked their money on it. All the later lenders and many of the early ones knew, also, that it was pledged for money to continue Spain's efforts to subdue a people struggling to free themselves from Spanish rule. They may have said the morality or justice of the use made of the money was no concern of theirs. They may have thought the security doubtful, and still relied on the broad guaranty of the Spanish nation. At any rate, caveat emptor! The one thing they ought not to have relied upon was that the island they were furnishing money to subdue, if it gained its freedom, would turn around and insist on reimbursing them!

The Spanish contention that it was in their power, as absolute sovereign of the struggling island, to fasten ineradicably upon it, for their own hostile purposes, unlimited claims to its future revenues, would lead to extraordinary results. Under that doctrine, any hard-pushed oppressor would have a certain means of subduing the most righteous revolt and condemning a colony to perpetual subjugation. He would only have to load it with bonds, issued for his own purposes, beyond any possible capacity it could ever have for payment. Under that load it could neither sustain itself independently, even if successful in war, nor persuade any other Power to accept responsibility for and control over it. It would be rendered impotent either for freedom or for any change of sovereignty. To ask the Nation sprung from the successful revolt of the thirteen colonies to acknowledge and act on an immoral doctrine like that, was, indeed, ingenuous—or audacious. The American Commissioners pronounced it alike repugnant to common sense and menacing to liberty and civilization. The Spanish Commissioners resented the characterization, but it is believed that the considerate judgment of the world will yet approve it. International practice will certainly hesitate hereafter, in transfers of sovereignty over territory after its successful revolt, at any recognition of loans negotiated by the ceding Power in its unsuccessful effort to subdue the revolt—no matter what pledges it had assumed to give about the future territorial revenues. Loans for the prosecution of unjust wars will be more sharply scrutinized in the money markets of the world, and will find less ready takers, however extravagant the rates. It may even happen that oppressing nations, in the increasing difficulty of floating such loans, will find it easier to relax the rigors of their rule and promote the orderly development of more liberal institutions among their subjects.

Far from being an encouragement, therefore, to repudiation, the American rejection of the so-called Cuban debt was a distinct contribution to international morality, and will probably furnish an important addition to International Law.

Ready to Pay Legitimate Colonial Debts.

At the same time the American Commissioners made clear in another case their sense of the duty to recognize any debt legitimately attaching to ceded territory. There was not the remotest thought of buying the Philippines, when a money payment was proposed, in that branch of the negotiations. When the Spanish fleet was sunk and the Spanish army captured at Manila, Spanish control over the Philippines was gone, and the Power that had destroyed it was compelled to assume its responsibilities to the civilized world at that commercial center and on that oceanic highway.[4] If that was not enough reason for the retention of the Philippines, then, at any rate, the right of the United States to them as indemnity for the war could not be contested by the generation which had witnessed the exaction of Alsace and Lorraine plus $1,000,000,000 indemnity for the Franco-Prussian War. The war with Spain had already cost the United States far above $300,000,000. When trying to buy Cuba from Spain, in the days of that island's greatest prosperity, the highest valuation the United States was ever willing to attach to it was $125,000,000. As an original proposition, nobody dreams that the American people would have consented to buy the remote Philippines at that figure or at the half of it. Who could think the Government exacting if it accepted them in lieu of a cash indemnity (which Spain was wholly incapable of paying) for a great deal more than double the value it had put upon Cuba, at its very doors?

It was certain, then, that the Philippines would be retained, unless the President and his Commissioners so construed their duty to protect their country's interests as to throw away, in advance of popular instruction, all possible chance of indemnity for the war. But there was an issue of Spanish bonds, called a Philippine loan, amounting to forty million dollars Mexican, or say a little less than twenty millions of American money. Warned by the results of inquiry as to the origin of the Cuban debt, the American Commissioners avoided undertaking to assume this en bloc. But in their first statement of the claim for cession of sovereignty in the Philippines, while intimating their belief in their absolute right to enforce the demand on the single ground of indemnity, they were careful to say that they were ready to stipulate "for the assumption of any existing indebtedness of Spain incurred for public works and improvements of a pacific character in the Philippines." When they learned that this entire "Philippine debt" had only been issued in 1897, that apparently a fourth had been transferred to Cuba to carry on the war against the Cuban insurgents, and finally against the United States, and that much of what was left of the remainder, after satisfying the demands of officials for "costs of negotiation," must have gone to the support of the government while engaged in prosecuting the war against the natives in Luzon, the American Commissioners abandoned the idea of assuming it. But even then they resolved, in the final transfer, to fix an amount at least equal to the face value of that debt, which could be given to Spain. She could use it to pay the Philippine bonds if she chose. Nothing further was said to Spain about the Philippine debt, and no specific reason for the payment was given in the ultimatum. The Commissioners merely observed that they "now present a new proposition, embodying the concessions which, for the sake of immediate peace, their Government is, under the circumstances, willing to tender." What had gone before showed plainly enough the American view as to the sanctity of public debt legitimately incurred in behalf of ceded territory, and explained the money payment in the case of the Philippines, as well as the precise amount at which it was finally fixed.

Privateering.

Neither the Peace of Paris nor the conflict which it closed can be said to have quite settled the status of private war at sea. "Privateering is and remains abolished," not in International Law, but merely between the Powers that signed that clause in the Declaration of Paris in 1856. But the greatest commercial nation, as well as the most powerful, that withheld its signature was the United States. Obviously its adhesion to the principle would bring more weight to the general acceptance among civilized nations, which is the essential for admission in International Law, than that of all the other dissenting nations.

Under these circumstances, the United States took the occasion of an outbreak of war between itself and another of the dissenting nations to announce that, for its part, it did not intend, under any circumstances, to resort to privateering. The other gave no such assurance, and was, in fact, expected (in accordance with frequent semi-official outgivings from Madrid) to commission privateers at an early day; but the disasters to its navy and the collapse of its finances left it without a safe opportunity. The moral effect of this volunteer action of the United States, with no offset of any active dissent by its opponent, becomes almost equivalent to completing that custom and assent of the civilized world which create International Law. Practically all governments may henceforth regard privateering as under international ban, and no one of the states yet refraining from assent—Spain, Mexico, Venezuela, or China—is likely to defy the ban. The announcement of the United States can probably be accepted as marking the end of private war at sea, and a genuine advance in the world's civilization.

Exempt all Private Property.

The refusal of the United States, in 1856, to join in the clause of the Declaration of Paris abolishing privateering was avowedly based upon the ground that it did not go far enough. The American claim was that not only private seizure of enemy's goods at sea should be prohibited, but that all private property of the enemy at sea should be entitled to the same protection as on land—prizes and prize courts being thus almost abolished, and no private property of the enemy anywhere being liable to confiscation, unless contraband of war. It was frankly stated at the time that without this addition the abolition of privateering was not in the interest of Powers like the United States, with a small navy, but a large and active merchant fleet. This peculiar adaptability of privateering at that time to the situation of the United States might have warranted the suspicion that its professions of a desire to make the Declaration of Paris broader than the other nations wished only masked a desire to have things remain as they were.

But the subsequent action of its Government in time of profound peace compelled a worthier view of its attitude. A treaty with Italy, negotiated by George P. Marsh, and ratified by the United States in 1871, embodied the very extension of the Declaration of Paris for which the United States contended. This treaty provides that "in the event of a war between them (Italy and the United States) the private property of their respective citizens and subjects, with the exception of contraband of war, shall be exempt from capture or seizure, on the high seas or elsewhere, by the armed vessels or by the military forces of either party." Is it too much to hope that this early committal of the United States with Italy, and its subsequent action in the war with Spain, may at last bring the world to the advanced ground it recommended for the Declaration of Paris, and throw the safeguards of civilization henceforth around all private property in time of war, whether on land or sea?

The Monroe Doctrine Stands.

Here, then, are three great principles, important to the advancement of civilization, which, if not established in International Law by the Peace of Paris and the war it closed, have at least been so powerfuly reinforced that no nation is likely hereafter lightly or safely to violate them.

But it has often been asked, and sometimes by eminent English writers, whether the Americans have not, at the same time, fatally unsettled the Monroe Doctrine, which never, indeed, had the sanction of International Law, but to which they were known to attach the greatest importance. A large and influential body of American opinion at first insisted that the acquisition of the West Indian, Philippine, and Sandwich Islands constituted an utter abandonment of that Doctrine; and apparently most European publicists have accepted this view. Only slight inquiry is needed to show that the facts give it little support.

The Monroe Doctrine sprang from the union of certain absolute monarchs (not claiming to rule by the will of the people, but by "divine right") in a "Holy Alliance" against that dangerous spread of democratic ideas which, starting in the revolt of the American colonies, had kindled the French Revolution and more or less unsettled government in Europe. It was believed that these monarchs meant not only to repress republican tendencies in Europe, but to assist Spain in reducing again to subjection American republics which had been established in former Spanish colonies, and had been recognized as independent by the United States. Under these circumstances, James Monroe, then President, in his Annual Message in 1823, formally announced the famous "Doctrine" in these words:

The occasion has been deemed proper for asserting as a principle in which the rights and interests of the United States are involved, that the American continents, by the free and independent condition which they have assumed and maintained, are henceforth not to be considered as subjects for future colonization by any European Powers.... Our policy in regard to Europe ... is not to interfere in the internal concerns of any of its Powers.

That is the whole substance of it. There was no pledge of abstention throughout the future and under all circumstances from the internal concerns of European Powers—only a statement of present practice. Far less was there a pledge, as seems to have been widely supposed, that if the Holy Alliance would only refrain from aiding Spain to force back the Mexican and South American republics into Spanish colonies, the United States would refrain from extending its institutions or its control over any region in Asia or Africa or the islands of the sea. Less yet was there any such talk as has been sometimes quoted, about keeping Europe out of the Western hemisphere and ourselves staying out of the Eastern hemisphere. What Mr. Monroe really said, in essence, was this: "The late Spanish colonies are now American republics, which we have recognized. They shall not be reduced to colonies again; and the two American continents have thus attained such an independent condition that they are no longer fields for European colonization." That fact remains. It does not seem probable that anybody will try or wish to change it. Furthermore, the United States has not interfered in the internal concerns of any European Powers. But it is under no direct pledge for the future to that effect; and as to Asia, Africa, and the islands of the sea, it is and always has been as free as anybody else. It encouraged and protected a colony on the west coast of Africa. It acquired the Aleutian Islands, largely in the Asiatic system. It long maintained a species of protectorate over the Sandwich Islands. It acquired an interest in Samoa and joined there in a protectorate. It has now taken the Sandwich Islands and the Philippines. Meanwhile the Monroe Doctrine remains just where it always was. Nothing has been done in contravention of it, and it stands as firmly as ever, though with the tragic end of the Franco-Austrian experiment in Mexico, and now with the final disappearance from the Western world of the unfortunate Power whose colonial experiences led to its original promulgation, the circumstances have so changed that nobody is very likely to have either interest or wish to interfere with it.

Leaving the Continent.

What has really been unsettled, if anything, by the Peace of Paris and the preceding war, has been the current American idea as to the sphere of national activities, and the power under the Constitution for their extension. It is perfectly true that the people did not wish for more territory, and never dreamed of distant colonies. There had always been a party that first opposed and then belittled the acquisition of Alaska. There was no considerable popular support since the Civil War for filibustering expeditions of the old sort against Cuba. There was genuine reluctance to take the steps which recent circumstances and the national committals for half a century made almost unavoidable in the Sandwich Islands. Now suddenly the United States found itself in possession of Cuba, Porto Rico, Guam, and the Philippines. The first impression was one of great popular perplexity. What was to be done with them? Must they be developed through the territorial stage into independent States in the Union? or, if not, how govern or get rid of them? What place was there in the American system for territories that were never to be States, for colonies, or for the rule of distant subject races?

Up to this time, from the outbreak of the war, the Administration had found the American people united in its support as they had hardly been united for a century. The South vied with the North, the West forgot the growing jealousy of the East, the poor the new antagonism to the rich, and the wildest cow-boys from Arizona and New Mexico marched fraternally beside scions of the oldest and richest families from New York, under the orders of a great Secessionist cavalry general.

But now two parties presently arose. One held that there was no creditable escape from the consequences of the war; that the Government, having broken down the existing authority in the capital of the Philippines, and practically throughout the archipelago, could neither set up that authority again nor shirk the duty of replacing it; that it was as easy and as constitutional to apply some modification of the existing territorial system to the Philippines as it had been to Alaska and the Aleutians; and that, while the task was no doubt disagreeable, difficult, and dangerous, it could not be avoided with honor, and would ultimately be attended with great profit. On the other hand, some prominent members of the Administration party led off in protests against the retention of the Philippines on constitutional, humanitarian, and economic grounds, pronouncing it a policy absolutely antagonistic to the principles of the Republic and the precursor of its downfall. In proportion as the Administration itself inclined to the former view, the opposition leaders fell away from the support they had given during the war, and began to align themselves with those members of the Administration party who had opposed the ratification of the treaty. They were reinforced by a considerable body of educated and conservative public opinion, chiefly at the East, and by a number of trades-union and labor leaders, who had been brought to believe that the new policy meant cheap labor and cheap manufactures in competition with their own, together with a large standing army, to which they have manifested great repugnance ever since the Chicago riots.

Anti-Administration View of the Constitution.

In the universal ferment of opinion and discussion that ensued, the opponents of what is assumed to be the Administration policy on the new possessions have seemed to rely chiefly on two provisions in the Constitution of the United States and a phrase in the Declaration of Independence. The constitutional provisions are:

The Congress shall have power to levy and collect taxes ... and provide for the common defense and general welfare of the United States; *but all duties, imposts, and excises shall be uniform throughout the United States.*—Art. I, Sec. 8.

All persons born or naturalized in the United States and subject to the jurisdiction thereof are citizens of the United States and of the State wherein they reside.—Art. XIV, Sec. 1.

To serve the purpose for which these clauses of the Constitution are invoked, it is necessary to hold that any territory to which the United States has a title is an integral part of the United States; and perhaps the greatest name in the history of American constitutional interpretation, that of Mr. Chief Justice Marshall of the Supreme Court of the United States, is cited in favor of that contention. If accepted, it follows that when the treaty ceding Spanish sovereignty in the Philippines was ratified, that archipelago became an integral part of the United States. Then, under the first clause above cited, the Dingley tariff must be immediately extended over the Philippines (as well as Porto Rico, the Sandwich Islands, and Guam) precisely as over New York; and, under the second clause, every native of the Philippines and the other new possessions is a citizen of the United States, with all the rights and privileges thereby accruing. The first result would be the disorganization of the present American revenue system by the free admission into all American ports of sugar and other tropical products from the greatest sources of supply, and the consequent loss of nearly sixty millions of annual revenue. Another would be the destruction of the existing cane- and beet-sugar industries in the United States. Another, apprehended by the laboring classes, who are already suspicious from their experience with the Chinese, would be an enormous influx, either of cheap labor or of its products, to beat down their wages.

Next, it is argued, there is no place in the theory or practice of the American Government for territories except for development into Statehood; and, consequently, the required population being already present, new States must be created out of Luzon, Mindanao, the Visayas, Porto Rico, and the Sandwich Islands. The right to hold them permanently in the territorial form, or even under a protectorate, is indignantly denied as conflicting with Mr. Jefferson's phrase in the Declaration of Independence, to the effect that governments derive their just powers from the consent of the governed. Some great names can certainly be marshaled in support of such views—Chancellor Kent, Mr. John C. Calhoun, Mr. Chief Justice Taney, and others. Denial of this duty to admit the new possessions as States is denounced as a violation by the Republic of the very law of its being, and its transformation into an empire; as a revival of slavery in another form, both because of government without representation, and because of the belief that no tropical colony can be successful without contract labor; as a consequent and inevitable degradation of American character; as a defiance of the warnings in Washington's Farewell Address against foreign entanglements; as a repudiation of the congressional declaration at the outbreak of the war, that it was not waged for territorial aggrandizement; and finally as placing Aguinaldo in the position of fighting for freedom, independence, and the principles of the fathers of the Republic, while the Republic itself is in the position of fighting to control and govern him and his people in spite of their will.

On the other hand, the supporters of the treaty and of the policy of the Administration, so far as it has been disclosed, begin their argument with another provision of the Constitution, the second part of Section 3 in Article IV:

The Congress shall have power to dispose of and make all needful rules and regulations respecting the territory or other property belonging to the United States.

They claim that, under this, Congress has absolute power to do what it will with the Philippines, as with any other territory or other property which the United States may acquire. It is admitted that Congress is, of course, under an implied obligation to exercise this power in the general spirit of the Constitution which creates it, and of the Government of which it is a part. But it is denied that Congress is under any obligation to confer a republican form of government upon a territory whose inhabitants are unfit for it, or to adopt any form of government devised with reference to preparing it for ultimate admission to the Union as a State.

It is further denied that Congress is under any obligation, arising either from the Constitution itself or from the precedents of the Nation's action under it, to ask the consent of the inhabitants in acquired territory to the form of government which may be given them. And still further, it is not only denied that Congress is under any obligations to prepare these territories for Statehood or admit them to it, but it is pointed out that, at least as to the Philippines, that body is prevented from doing so by the very terms, of the preamble to the Constitution itself—concluding with the words, "do ordain and establish this Constitution for the United States *of America*." There is no place here for States of Asia.

Replies to Constitutional Objections.

In dealing with the arguments against retention of the Philippines, based on the sections previously quoted from Articles I and XIV of the Constitution, the friends of the policy say that the apparent conflict in these articles with the wide grant of powers over territory to Congress which they find in Article IV arises wholly from a failure to recognize the different senses in which the term "the United States" is used. As the name of the Nation it is often employed to include all territory over which United States sovereignty extends, whether originally the property of the individual States and ceded to the United States, or whether acquired in treaties by the Nation itself. But such a meaning is clearly inconsistent with its use in certain clauses of the Constitution in question. Thus Article XIII says: "Neither slavery nor involuntary servitude ... shall exist within the United States *or any place subject to their jurisdiction*."

The latter clause was obviously the constitutional way of conveying the idea about the Territories which the opponents of the Philippine policy are now trying to read into the name "United States." The constitutional provision previously cited about citizenship illustrates the same point. It says "all persons born," etc., "are citizens of the United States *and of the State wherein they reside*." There is no possibility left here that Territories are to be held as an integral part of the United States, in the sense in which the Constitution, in this clause, uses the name. If they had been, the clause would have read, "and of the State *or Territory* in which they reside." For these opinions high authorities are also cited, including debates in the Senate, acts of Congress, the constant practice of the Executive, and most of the judicial rulings of the last half-century that seem to bear upon the present situation.

The Outcome not Doubtful.

It has been thought best, in an explanation to readers in another country of the perplexity arising in the American mind, in a sudden emergency, from these disputed points in constitutional powers, to set forth with impartial fairness and some precision the views on either side. It is essential to a fair judgment as to the apparent hesitation since this problem began to develop, that the real basis for the conflicting opinions should be understood, and that full justice should be done to the earnest repugnance with which many conscientious citizens draw back from sending American youth to distant tropical regions to enforce with an armed hand the submission of an unwilling people to the absolute rule of the Republic. It should be realized, too, how far the new departure does unsettle the practice and policy of a century. The old view that each new Territory is merely another outlet for surplus population, soon to be taken in as another State in the Union, must be abandoned. The old assumption that all inhabitants of territory belonging to the United States are to be regarded as citizens is gone. The idea that government anywhere must derive its just powers only from the consent of the governed is unsettled, and thus, to some, the very foundations of the Republic seem to be shaken. Three generations, trained in Washington's warnings against foreign entanglements, find it difficult all at once to realize that advice adapted to a people of three millions, scattered along the border of a continent, may need some modifications when applied to a people of seventy-five millions, occupying the continent, and reaching out for the commerce of both the oceans that wash its shores.

But whatever may be thought of the weight of the argument, either as to constitutional power or as to policy, there is little doubt as to the result. The people who found authority in their fundamental law for treating paper currency as a legal tender in time of war, in spite of the constitutional requirement that no State should "make anything but gold and silver coin a tender in payment of debts," will find there also all the power they need for dealing with the difficult problem that now confronts them. And when the constitutional objections are surmounted, those as to policy are not likely to lead the American people to recall their soldiers from the fields on which the Filipinos attacked them, or abandon the sovereignty which Spain ceded. The American Government has the new territories, and will hold and govern them.

A republic like the United States has not been well adapted hitherto to that sort of work. Congress is apt to be slow, if not also changeable, and under the Constitution the method of government for territories must be prescribed by Congress. It has not yet found time to deal with the Sandwich Islands. Its harsher critics declare it has never yet found time to deal fairly with Alaska. No doubt, Executive action in advance of Congress might be satisfactory; but a President is apt to wait for Congress unless driven by irresistible necessities. He can only take the initiative through some form of military government. For this the War Department is not yet well organized. Possibly the easiest solution for the moment would be in the organization of another department for war and government beyond the seas, or the development of a measurably independent bureau for such work in the present department. Whatever is done, it would be unreasonable to expect unbroken success or exemption from a learner's mistakes and discouragements. But whoever supposes that these will result either in the abandonment of the task or in a final failure with it does not know the American people.

VII

OUR NEW DUTIES

This commencement address was delivered on the campus at Miami University, Oxford, Ohio, at the celebration of its seventy-fifth anniversary, June 15, 1899.

OUR NEW DUTIES

Sons and Friends of Miami: I join you in saluting this venerable mother at a notable waymark in her great life. One hundred and seven years ago the Congress voted, and George Washington approved, a foundation for this University. Seventy-five years ago it opened its doors. Now, si monumentum quæris, circumspice. There is the catalogue. There are the long lists of men who so served the State or the Church that their lives are your glory, their names your inspiration.[5] There are the longer lists of others to whom kinder fortune did not set duties in the eye of the world; but Miami made of them citizens who leavened the lump of that growing West which was then a sprawling, irregular line of pioneer settlements, and is now an empire. Search through it, above and below the Ohio, and beyond the Mississippi. So often, where there are centers of good work or right thinking and right living—so often and so widely spread will you find traces of Miami, left by her own sons or coming from those secondary sources which sprang from her example and influence, that you are led in grateful surprise to exclaim: "If this be the work of a little college, God bless and prolong the little college! If, half starved and generally neglected, she has thus nourished good learning and its proper result in good lives through the three quarters of a century ended to-day, may the days of her years be as the sands of the sea; may the Twentieth Century only introduce the glorious prime of a career of which the Nineteenth saw but modest beginnings, and may good old Miami still flourish in sæcula sæculorum!"

But the celebration of her past and the aspirations for her future belong to worthier sons—here among these gentlemen of the Board who have cared for her in her need. I make them my profound acknowledgments for the honor they have done me in assigning me a share in the work of this day of days, and shall best deserve their trust by going with absolute candor straight to my theme.

New Duties; a New World.

I shall speak of the new duties that are upon us and the new world that is opening to us with the new century—of the spirit in which we should advance and the results we have the right to ask. I shall speak of public matters which it is the duty of educated men to consider; and of matters which may hereafter divide parties, but on which we must refuse now to recognize party distinctions. Partizanship stops at the guard-line. "In the face of an enemy we are all Frenchmen," said an eloquent Imperialist once in my hearing, in rallying his followers to support a foreign measure of the French Republic. At this moment our soldiers are facing a barbarous or semi-civilized foe, who treacherously attacked them in a distant land, where our flag had been sent, in friendship with them, for the defense of our own shores. Was it creditable or seemly that it was lately left to a Bonaparte on our own soil to teach some American leaders that, at such a time, patriotic men at home do not discourage those soldiers or weaken the Government that directs them?[6]

Neither shall I discuss, here and now, the wisdom of all the steps that have led to the present situation. For good or ill, the war was fought. Its results are upon us. With the ratification of the Peace of Paris, our Continental Republic has stretched its wings over the West Indies and the East. It is a fact and not a theory that confronts us. We are actually and now responsible, not merely to the inhabitants and to our own people, but, in International Law, to the commerce, the travel, the civilization of the world, for the preservation of order and the protection of life and property in Cuba, in Porto Rico, in Guam, and in the Philippine Archipelago, including that recent haunt of piracy, the Sulus. Shall we quit ourselves like men in the discharge of this immediate duty; or shall we fall to quarreling with each other like boys as to whether such a duty is a good or a bad thing for the country, and as to who got it fastened upon us? There may have been a time for disputes about the wisdom of resisting the stamp tax, but it was not just after Bunker Hill. There may have been a time for hot debate about some mistakes in the antislavery agitation, but not just after Sumter and Bull Run. Furthermore, it is as well to remember that you can never grind with the water that has passed the mill. Nothing in human power can ever restore the United States to the position it occupied the day before Congress plunged us into the war with Spain, or enable us to escape what that war entailed. No matter what we wish, the old continental isolation is gone forever. Whithersoever we turn now, we must do it with the burden of our late acts to carry, the responsibility of our new position to assume.

When the sovereignty which Spain had exercised with the assent of all nations over vast and distant regions for three hundred years was solemnly transferred under the eye of the civilized world to the United States, our first responsibility became the restoration of order. Till that is secured, any hindrance to the effort is bad citizenship—as bad as resistance to the police; as much worse, in fact, as its consequences may be more bloody and disastrous. "You have a wolf by the ears," said an accomplished ex-Minister of the United States to a departing Peace Commissioner last autumn. "You cannot let go of him with either dignity or safety, and he will not be easy to tame."

Policy for the New Possessions.

But when the task is accomplished,—when the Stars and Stripes at last bring the order and peaceful security they typify, instead of wanton disorder, with all the concomitants of savage warfare over which they now wave,—we shall then be confronted with the necessity of a policy for the future of these distant regions. It is a problem that calls for our soberest, most dispassionate, and most patriotic thought. The colleges, and the educated classes generally, should make it a matter of conscience—painstakingly considered on all its sides, with reference to International Law, the burdens of sovereignty, the rights and the interests of native tribes, and the legitimate demands of civilization—to find first our national duty and then our national interest, which it is also a duty for our statesmen to protect. On such a subject we have a right to look to our colleges for the help they should be so well equipped to give. From these still regions of cloistered thought may well come the white light of pure reason, not the wild, whirling words of the special pleader or of the partizan, giving loose rein to his hasty first impressions. It would be an ill day for some colleges if crude and hot-tempered incursions into current public affairs, like a few unhappily witnessed of late, should lead even their friends to fear lest they have been so long accustomed to dogmatize to boys that they have lost the faculty of reasoning with men.

When the first duty is done, when order is restored in those commercial centers and on that commercial highway, somebody must then be responsible for maintaining it—either ourselves or some Power whom we persuade to take them off our hands. Does anybody doubt what the American people in their present temper would say to the latter alternative?—the same people who, a fortnight ago, were ready to break off their Joint Commission with Great Britain and take the chances, rather than give up a few square miles of worthless land and a harbor of which a year ago they scarcely knew the name, on the remote coast of Alaska. Plainly it is idle now, in a government so purely dependent on the popular will, to scheme or hope for giving the Philippine task over to other hands as soon as order is restored. We must, then, be prepared with a policy for maintaining it ourselves.

Of late years men have unthinkingly assumed that new territory is, in the very nature of our Government, merely and necessarily the raw material for future States in the Union. Colonies and dependencies, it is now said, are essentially inconsistent with our system. But if any ever entertained the wild dream that the instrument whose preamble says it is ordained for the United States of *America* could be stretched to the China Sea, the first Tagal guns fired at friendly soldiers of the Union, and the first mutilation of American dead that ensued, ended the nightmare of States from Asia admitted to the American Union. For that relief, at least, we must thank the uprising of the Tagals. It was a Continental Union of independent sovereign States our fathers planned. Whoever proposes to debase it with admixtures of States made up from the islands of the sea, in any archipelago, East or West, is a bad friend to the Republic. We may guide, protect, elevate them, and even teach them some day to stand alone; but if we ever invite them into our Senate and House, to help to rule us, we are the most imbecile of all the offspring of time.

The Constitutional Objection.

Yet we must face the fact that able and conscientious men believe the United States has no constitutional power to hold territory that is not to be erected into States in the Union, or to govern people that are not to be made citizens. They are able to cite great names in support of their contention; and it would be an ill omen for the freest and most successful constitutional government in the world if a constitutional objection thus fortified should be carelessly considered or hastily overridden. This objection rests mainly on the assumption that the name "United States," as used in the Constitution, necessarily includes all territory the Nation owns, and on the historic fact that large parts of this territory, on acquiring sufficient population, have already been admitted as States, and have generally considered such admission to be a right. Now, Mr. Chief Justice Marshall—than whom no constitutional authority carries greater weight—certainly did declare that the question what was designated by the term "United States" in the clause of the Constitution giving power to levy duties on imposts "admitted of but one answer." It "designated the whole of the American empire, composed of States and Territories." If that be accepted as final, then the tariff must be applied in Manila precisely as in New York, and goods from Manila must enter the New York custom-house as freely as goods from New Orleans. Sixty millions would disappear instantly and annually from the Treasury, and our revenue system would be revolutionized by the free admission of sugar and other tropical products from the United States of Asia and the Caribbean Sea; while, on the other hand, the Philippines themselves would be fatally handicapped by a tariff wholly unnatural to their locality and circumstances. More. If that be final, the term "United States" should have the same comprehensive meaning in the clause as to citizenship. Then Aguinaldo is to-day a citizen of the United States, and may yet run for the Presidency. Still more. The Asiatics south of the China Sea are given that free admission to the country which we so strenuously deny to Asiatics from the north side of the same sea. Their goods, produced on wages of a few cents a day, come into free competition in all our home markets with the products of American labor, and the cheap laborers themselves are free to follow if ever our higher wages attract them. More yet. If that be final, the Tagals and other tribes of Luzon, the Visayans of Negros and Cebu, and the Mohammedan Malays of Mindanao and the Sulus, having each far more than the requisite population, may demand admission next winter into the Union as free and independent States, with representatives in Senate and House, and may plausibly claim that they can show a better title to admission than Nevada ever did, or Utah or Idaho.

Nor does the great name of Marshall stand alone in support of such conclusions. The converse theory that these territories are not necessarily included in the constitutional term "the United States" makes them our subject dependencies, and at once the figure of Jefferson himself is evoked, with all the signers of the immortal Declaration grouped about him, renewing the old war-cry that government derives its just powers from the consent of the governed. At different periods in our history eminent statesmen have made protests on grounds of that sort. Even the first bill for Mr. Jefferson's own purchase of Louisiana was denounced by Mr. Macon as "establishing a species of government unknown to the United States"; by Mr. Lucas as "establishing elementary principles never previously introduced in the government of any Territory of the United States"; and by Mr. Campbell as "really establishing a complete despotism." In 1823 Chancellor Kent said, with reference to Columbia River settlements, that "a government by Congress as absolute sovereign, over colonies, absolute dependents, was not congenial to the free and independent spirit of American institutions." In 1848 John C. Calhoun declared that "the conquest and retention of Mexico as a province would be a departure from the settled policy of the Government, in conflict with its character and genius, and in the end subversive of our free institutions." In 1857 Mr. Chief Justice Taney said that "a power to rule territory without restriction as a colony or dependent province would be inconsistent with the nature of our Government." And now, following warily in this line, the eminent and trusted advocate of similar opinions to-day, Mr. Senator Hoar of Massachusetts, says: "The making of new States and providing national defense are constitutional ends, so that we may acquire and hold territory for those purposes. The governing of subject peoples is not a constitutional end, and there is therefore no constitutional warrant for acquiring and holding territory for that purpose."

An Alleged Constitutional Inability.

We have now, as is believed, presented with entire fairness a summary of the more important aspects in which the constitutional objections mentioned have been urged. I would not underrate by a hair's breadth the authority of these great names, the weight of these continuous reassertions of principle, the sanction even of the precedent and general practice through a century. And yet I venture to think that no candid and competent man can thoroughly investigate the subject, in the light of the actual provisions of the Constitution, the avowed purpose of its framers, their own practice and the practice of their successors, without being absolutely convinced that this whole fabric of opposition on constitutional grounds is as flimsy as a cobweb. This country of our love and pride is no malformed, congenital cripple of a nation, incapable of undertaking duties that have been found within the powers of every other nation that ever existed since governments among civilized men began. Neither by chains forged in the Constitution nor by chains of precedent, neither by the dead hand we all revere, that of the Father of his Country, nor under the most authoritative exponents of our organic act and of our history, are we so bound that we cannot undertake any duty that devolves or exercise any power which the emergency demands. Our Constitution has entrapped us in no impasse, where retreat is disgrace and advance is impossible. The duty which the hand of Providence, rather than any purpose of man, has laid upon us, is within our constitutional powers. Let me invoke your patience for a rather minute and perhaps wearisome detail of the proof.

The notion that the United States is an inferior sort of nation, constitutionally without power for such public duties as other nations habitually assume, may perhaps be dismissed with a single citation from the Supreme Court. Said Mr. Justice Bradley, in the Legal Tender Cases: "As a government it [the United States] was invested with all the attributes of sovereignty.... It seems to be a self-evident proposition that it is invested with all those inherent and implied powers which, at the time of adopting the Constitution, were generally considered to belong to every government as such, and as being essential to the exercise of its functions" (12 Wall. 554).

Every one recalls this constitutional provision: "The Congress shall have power to dispose of and make all needful rules and regulations respecting the territory or other property of the United States." That grant is absolute, and the only qualification is the one to be drawn from the general spirit of the Government the Constitution was framed to organize. Is it consistent with that spirit to hold territory permanently, or for long periods of time, without admitting it to the Union? Let the man who wrote the very clause in question answer. That man was Gouverneur Morris of New York, and you will find his answer on page 192 of the third volume of his writings, given only fifteen years after, in reply to a direct question as to the exact meaning of the clause: "I always thought, when we should acquire Canada and Louisiana, it would be proper to govern them as provinces, and allow them no voice in our councils. In wording the third section of the fourth article, I went as far as circumstances would permit to establish the exclusion." This framer of the Constitution desired then, and intended definitely and permanently, to keep *Louisiana* out! And yet there are men who tell us the provision he drew would not even permit us to keep the Philippines out! To be more papist than the Pope will cease to be a thing exciting wonder if every day modern men, in the consideration of practical and pressing problems, are to be more narrowly constitutional than the men that wrote the Constitution!

Is it said that, at any rate, our practice under this clause of the Constitution has been against the view of the man that wrote it, and in favor of that quoted from Mr. Chief Justice Marshall? Does anybody seriously think, then, that though we have held New Mexico, Arizona, and Oklahoma as territory organized or unorganized, part of it nearly a century and all of it half a century, our representatives believed all the while they had no constitutional right to do so? Who imagines that when the third of a century during which we have already held Alaska is rounded out to a full century, that unorganized Territory will even then have any greater prospect than at present of admission as a State? or who believes our grandchildren will be violating the Constitution in keeping it out? Who imagines that under the Constitution ordained on this continent specifically "for the United States of *America,*" we will ever permit the Kanakas, Chinese, and Japanese, who make up a majority of the population in the Sandwich Islands, to set up a government of their own and claim admission as an independent and sovereign State of our American Union? Finally, let me add that conclusive proof relating not only to practice under the Constitution, but to the precise construction of the constitutional language as to the Territories by the highest authority, in the light of long previous practice, is to be found in another part of the instrument itself, deliberately added three quarters of a century later. Article XIII provides that "neither slavery nor involuntary servitude shall exist within the United States, *or any place subject to their jurisdiction*." If the term "the United States," as used in the Constitution, really includes the Territories as an integral part, as Mr. Chief Justice Marshall said, what, then, does the Constitution mean by the additional words, "or any place subject to their jurisdiction"? Is it not too plain for argument that the Constitution here refers to territory not a part of the United States, but subject to its jurisdiction—territory, for example, like the Sandwich Islands or the Philippines?

What, then, shall we say to the opinion of the great Chief Justice?—for, after all, his is not a name to be dealt with lightly. Well, first, it was a dictum, not a decision of the court. Next, in another and later case, before the same eminent jurist, came a constitutional expounder as eminent and as generally accepted,—none other than Daniel Webster,—who took precisely the opposite view. He was discussing the condition of certain territory on this continent which we had recently acquired. Said Mr. Webster: "What is Florida? It is no part of the United States. How can it be? Florida is to be governed by Congress as it thinks proper. Congress might have done anything—might have refused a trial by jury, and refused a legislature." After this flat contradiction of the court's former dictum, what happened? Mr. Webster won his case, and the Chief Justice made not the slightest reference to his own previous and directly conflicting opinion! Need we give it more attention now than Marshall did then?

Mr. Webster maintained the same position long afterward, in the Senate of the United States, in opposition to Mr. John C. Calhoun, and his view has been continuously sustained since by the courts and by congressional action. In the debate with Mr. Calhoun in February, 1849, Mr. Webster said: "What is the Constitution of the United States? Is not its very first principle that all within its influence and comprehension shall be represented in the Legislature which it establishes, with not only a right of debate and a right to vote in both houses of Congress, but a right to partake in the choice of President and Vice-President?... The President of the United

States shall govern this territory as he sees fit till Congress makes further provision.... We have never had a territory governed as the United States is governed.... I do not say that while we sit here to make laws for these territories, we are not bound by every one of those great principles which are intended as general securities for public liberty. But they do not exist in territories till introduced by the authority of Congress.... Our history is uniform in its course. It began with the acquisition of Louisiana. It went on after Florida became a part of the Union. In all cases, under all circumstances, by every proceeding of Congress on the subject and by all judicature on the subject, it has been held that territories belonging to the United States were to be governed by a constitution of their own,... and in approving that constitution the legislation of Congress was not necessarily confined to those principles that bind it when it is exercised in passing laws for the United States itself." Mr. Calhoun, in the course of this debate, asked Mr. Webster for judicial opinion sustaining these views, and Mr. Webster said that "the same thing has been decided by the United States courts over and over again for the last thirty years."

I may add that it has been so held over and over again during the subsequent fifty. Mr. Chief Justice Waite, giving the opinion of the Supreme Court of the United States (in National Bank *v.* County of Yankton, 101 U.S. 129-132), said: "It is certainly now too late to doubt the power of Congress to govern the Territories. Congress is supreme, and, for all the purposes of this department, has all the powers of the people of the United States, except such as have been expressly or by implication reserved in the prohibitions of the Constitution."

Mr. Justice Stanley Matthews of the United States Supreme Court stated the same view with even greater clearness in one of the Utah polygamy cases (Murphy *v.* Ramsey, 114 U.S. 44, 45): "It rests with Congress to say whether in a given case any of the people resident in the Territory shall participate in the election of its officers or the making of its laws. It may take from them any right of suffrage it may previously have conferred, or at any time modify or abridge it, as it may deem expedient.... Their political rights are franchises which they hold as privileges, in the legislative discretion of the United States."

The very latest judicial utterance on the subject is in harmony with all the rest. Mr. Justice Morrow of the United States Court of Appeals for the Ninth Circuit, in February, 1898, held (57 U.S. Appeals 6): "The now well-established doctrine [is] that the Territories of the United States are entirely subject to the legislative authority of Congress. They are not organized under the Constitution nor subject to its complex distribution of the powers of government. The United States, having rightfully acquired the Territories, and being the only Government which can impose laws upon them, has the entire dominion and sovereignty, national and municipal, Federal and State."

More Recent Constitutional Objections.

In the light of such expositions of our constitutional power and our uniform national practice, it is difficult to deal patiently with the remaining objections to the acquisition of territory, purporting to be based on constitutional grounds. One is that to govern the Philippines without their consent or against the opposition of Aguinaldo is to violate the principle—only formulated, to be sure, in the Declaration of Independence, but, as they say, underlying the whole Constitution—that government derives its just powers from the consent of the governed. In the Sulu group piracy prevailed for centuries. How could a government that put it down rest on the consent of Sulu? Would it be without just powers because the pirates did not vote in its favor? In other parts of the archipelago what has been stigmatized as a species of slavery prevails. Would a government that stopped that be without just powers till the slaveholders had conferred them at a popular election? In another part head-hunting is, at certain seasons of the year, a recognized tribal custom. Would a government that interfered with that practice be open to denunciation as an usurpation, without just powers, and flagrantly violating the Constitution of the United States, unless it waited at the polls for the consent of the head-hunters? The truth is, all intelligent men know—and few even in America, except obvious demagogues, hesitate to admit—that there are cases where a good government does not and ought not to rest on the consent of the governed. If men will not govern themselves with respect for civilization and its agencies, then when they get in the way they must be governed—always have been, whenever the world was not retrograding, and always will be. The notion that such government is a revival of slavery, and that the United States by doing its share of such work in behalf of civilization would therefore become infamous, though put forward with apparent gravity in some eminently respectable quarters, is too fantastic for serious consideration.

Mr. Jefferson may be supposed to have known the meaning of the words he wrote. Instead of vindicating a righteous rebellion in the Declaration, he was called, after a time, to exercise a righteous government under the Constitution. Did he himself, then, carry his own words to such extremes as these professed disciples now demand? Was he guilty of subverting the principles of the Government in buying some hundreds of thousands of Spaniards, Frenchmen, Creoles, and Indians, "like sheep in the shambles," as the critics untruthfully say we did in the Philippines? We bought nobody there. We held the Philippines first by the same right by which we held our own original thirteen States,—the oldest and firmest of all rights, the right by which nearly every great nation holds the bulk of its territory,—the right of conquest. We held them again as a rightful indemnity, and a low one, for a war in which the vanquished could give no other. We bought nothing; and the twenty millions that accompanied the transfer just balanced the Philippine debt.

But Jefferson did, if you choose to accept the hypercritical interpretation of these latter-day Jeffersonians—Jefferson did buy the Louisianians, even "like sheep in the shambles," if you care so to describe it; and did proceed to govern them without the consent of the governed. Monroe bought the Floridians without their consent. Polk conquered the Californians, and Pierce bought the New Mexicans. Seward bought the Russians and Alaskans, and we have governed them ever since, without their consent. Is it easy, in the face of such facts, to preserve your respect for an objection so obviously captious as that based on the phrase from the Declaration of Independence?

Nor is the turn Senator Hoar gives the constitutional objection much more weighty. He wishes to take account of motives, and pry into the purpose of those concerned in any acquisition of territory, before the tribunals can decide whether it is constitutional or not. If acquired either for the national defense or to be made a State, the act is constitutional; otherwise not. If, then, Jefferson intended to make a State out of Idaho, his act in acquiring that part of the Louisiana Purchase was all right. Otherwise he violated the Constitution he had helped to make and sworn to uphold. And yet, poor man, he hardly knew of the existence of that part of the territory, and certainly never dreamed that it would ever become a State, any more than Daniel Webster dreamed, to quote his own language in the Senate, that "California would ever be worth a dollar." Is Gouverneur Morris to be arraigned as false to the Constitution he helped to frame because he wanted to acquire Louisiana and Canada, and keep them both out of the Union? Did Mr. Seward betray the Constitution and violate his oath in buying Alaska without the purpose of making it a State? It seems—let it be said with all respect—that we have reached the reductio ad absurdum, and that the constitutional argument in any of its phases need not be further pursued.

The Little Americans.

If I have wearied you with these detailed proofs of a doctrine which Mr. Justice Morrow rightly says is now well established, and these replies to its assailants, the apology must be found in the persistence with which the utter lack of constitutional power to deal with our new possessions has been vociferously urged from the outset by the large class of our people whom I venture to designate as the Little Americans, using that term not in the least in disparagement, but solely as distinctive and convenient. From the beginning of the century, at every epoch in our history we have had these Little Americans. They opposed Jefferson as to getting Louisiana. They opposed Monroe as to Florida. They were vehement against Texas, against California, against organizing Oregon and Washington, against the Gadsden Purchase, against Alaska, and against the Sandwich Islands. At nearly every stage in that long story of expansion the Little Americans have either denied the constitutional authority to acquire and govern, or denounced the acquisitions as worthless and dangerous. At one stage, indeed, they went further. When State after State was passing ordinances of secession, they raised the cry,—erroneously attributed to my distinguished predecessor and friend, Horace Greeley, but really uttered by Winfield Scott,—"Wayward Sisters, depart in peace!" Happily, this form, too, of Little Americanism failed. We are all glad now,—my distinguished classmate here,[7] who wore the gray and invaded Ohio with Morgan, as glad as myself,—we all rejoice that these doctrines were then opposed and overborne. It was seen then, and I venture to think it may be seen now, that it is a fundamental principle with the American people, and a duty imposed upon all who represent them, to maintain the Continental Union of American Independent States in all the purity of the fathers' conception; to hold what belongs to it, and get what it is entitled to; and, finally, that wherever its flag has been rightfully advanced, there it is to be kept. If that be Imperialism, make the most of it!

The Plain Path of Duty.

It was no vulgar lust of power that inspired the statesmen and soldiers of the Republic when they resisted the halting counsel of the Little Americans in the past. Nor is it now. Far other is the spirit we invoke:

> Stern daughter of the Voice of God,
>
> O Duty! If that name thou love—

in that name we beg for a study of what the new situation that is upon us, the new world opening around us, now demand at our hands.

The people of the United States will not refuse an appeal in that name. They never have. They had been so occupied, since the Civil War, first in repairing its ravages, and then in occupying and possessing their own continent, they had been so little accustomed, in this generation or the last, to even the thought of foreign war, that one readily understands why at the outset they hardly realized how absolute is the duty of an honorable conqueror to accept and discharge the responsibilities of his conquest. But this is no longer a child-nation, irresponsible in its nonage and incapable of comprehending or assuming the responsibilities of its acts. A child that breaks a pane of glass or sets fire to a house may indeed escape. Are we to plead the baby act, and claim that we can flounce around the world, breaking international china and burning property, and yet repudiate the bill because we have not come of age? Who dare say that a self-respecting Power could have sailed away from Manila and repudiated the responsibilities of its victorious belligerency? After going into a war for humanity, were we so craven that we should seek freedom from further trouble at the expense of civilization?

If we did not want those responsibilities we ought not to have gone to war, and I, for one, would have been content. But having chosen to go to war, and having been speedily and overwhelmingly successful, we should be ashamed even to think of running away from what inexorably followed. Mark what the successive steps were, and how link by link the chain that binds us now was forged.

The moment war was foreseen the fleet we usually have in Chinese waters became indispensable, not merely, as before, to protect our trade and our missionaries in China, but to checkmate the Spanish fleet, which otherwise held San Francisco and the whole Pacific coast at its mercy. When war was declared our fleet was necessarily ordered out of neutral ports. Then it had to go to Manila or go home. If it went home, it left the whole Pacific coast unguarded, save at the particular point it touched, and we should have been at once in a fever of apprehension, chartering hastily another fleet of the fastest ocean-going steamers we could find in the world, to patrol the Pacific from San Diego to Sitka, as we did have to patrol the Atlantic from Key West to Bar Harbor. Palpably this was to go the longest way around to do a task that had to be done in any event, as well as to demoralize our forces at the opening of the war with a manœuver in which our Navy has never been expert—that of avoiding a contest and sailing away from the enemy! The alternative was properly taken. Dewey went to Manila and sank the Spanish fleet. We thus broke down Spanish means for controlling the Philippines, and were left with the Spanish responsibility for maintaining order there—responsibility to all the world, German, English, Japanese, Russian, and the rest—in one of the great centers and highways of the world's commerce.

But why not turn over that commercial center and the island on which it is situated to the Tagals? To be sure! Under three hundred years of Spanish rule barbarism on Luzon had so far disappeared that this commercial metropolis, as large as San Francisco or Cin-

cinnati, had sprung up and come to be thronged by traders and travelers of all nations. Now it is calmly suggested that we might have turned it over to one semi-civilized tribe, absolutely without experience in governing even itself, much less a great community of foreigners, probably in a minority on the island, and at war with its other inhabitants—a tribe which has given the measure of its fitness for being charged with the rights of foreigners and the care of a commercial metropolis by the violation of flags of truce, treachery to the living, and mutilation of the dead which have marked its recent wanton rising against the Power that was trying to help it!

If running away from troublesome responsibility and duty is our rôle, why did we not long ago take the opportunity, in our early feebleness, to turn over Tallahassee and St. Augustine to the Seminoles, instead of sending Andrew Jackson to protect the settlements and subdue the savages? Why, at the first Apache outbreak after the Gadsden Purchase, did we not hasten to turn over New Mexico and Arizona to *their* inhabitants? Or why, in years within the memory of most of you, when the Sioux and Chippewas rose on our Northwestern frontier, did we not invite them to retain possession of St. Cloud, and even come down, if they liked, to St. Paul and Minneapolis?

Unless I am mistaken in regarding all these suggestions as too unworthy to be entertained by self-respecting citizens of a powerful and self-respecting nation, we have now reached two conclusions that ought to clear the air and simplify the problem that remains: First, we have ample constitutional power to acquire and govern new territory absolutely at will, according to our sense of right and duty, whether as dependencies, as colonies, or as a protectorate. Secondly, as the legitimate and necessary consequence of our own previous acts, it has become our national and international duty to do it.

The Policy for our Dependencies

How shall we set about it? What shall be the policy with which, when order has been inexorably restored, we begin our dealings with the new wards of the Nation? Certainly we must mark our disapproval of the treachery and barbarities of the present contest. As certainly the oppression of other tribes by the Tagals must be ended, or the oppression of any tribe by any other within the sphere of our active control. Wars between the tribes must be discouraged and prevented. We must seek to suppress crimes of violence and private vengeance, secure individual liberty, protect individual property, and promote the study of the arts of peace. Above all, we must give and enforce justice; and for the rest, as far as possible, leave them alone. By all means let us avoid a fussy meddling with their customs, manners, prejudices, and beliefs. Give them order and justice, and trust to these to win them in other regards to our ways. All this points directly to utilizing existing agencies as much as possible, developing native initiative and control in local matters as fast and as far as we can, and ultimately giving them the greatest degree of self-government for which they prove themselves fitted.

Under any conditions that exist now, or have existed for three hundred years, a homogeneous native government over the whole archipelago is obviously impossible. Its relations to the outside world must necessarily be assumed by us. We must preserve order in Philippine waters, regulate the harbors, fix and collect the duties, apportion the revenue, and supervise the expenditure. We must enforce sanitary measures. We must retain such a control of the superior courts as shall make justice certainly attainable, and such control of the police as shall insure its enforcement. But in all this, after the absolute authority has been established, the further the natives can themselves be used to carry out the details, the better.

Such a system might not be unwise even for a colony to which we had reason to expect a considerable emigration of our own people. If experience of a kindred nation in dealing with similar problems counts for anything, it is certainly wise for a distant dependency, always to be populated mainly, save in the great cities, by native races, and little likely ever to be quite able to stand alone, while, nevertheless, we wish to help it just as much as possible to that end.

The Duty of Public Servants.

Certainly this is no bed of flowery ease in the dreamy Orient to which we are led. No doubt these first glimpses of the task that lies before us, as well as the warfare with distant tribes into which we have been unexpectedly plunged, will provoke for the time a certain discontent with our new possessions. But on a far-reaching question of national policy the wise public man is not so greatly disturbed by what people say in momentary discouragement under the first temporary check. That which really concerns him is what people at a later day, or even in a later generation, might say of men trusted with great duties for their country, who proved unequal to their opportunities, and through some short-sighted timidity of the moment lost the chance of centuries.

It is quite true, as was recently reported in what seemed an authoritative way from Washington, that the Peace Commissioners were not entirely of one mind at the outset, and equally true that the final conclusion at Washington was apparently reached on the Commission's recommendation from Paris. As the cold fit, in the language of one of our censors, has followed the hot fit in the popular temper, I readily take the time which hostile critics consider unfavorable, for accepting my own share of responsibility, and for avowing for myself that I declared my belief in the duty and policy of holding the whole Philippine Archipelago in the very first conference of the Commissioners in the President's room at the White House, in advance of any instructions of any sort. If vindication for it be needed, I confidently await the future.

What *is* the duty of a public servant as to profiting by opportunities to secure for his country what all the rest of the world considers material advantages? Even if he could persuade himself that rejecting them is morally and internationally admissible, is he at liberty to commit his country irrevocably to their rejection, because they do not wholly please his individual fancy? At a former negotiation of our own in Paris, the great desire of the United States representative, as well as of his Government, had been mainly to secure the settled or partly settled country adjoining us on the south, stretching from the Floridas to the city of New Orleans. The possession of the vast unsettled and unknown Louisiana Territory, west of the Mississippi, was neither sought nor thought of. Suddenly, on an eventful morning in April, 1803, Talleyrand astonished Livingston by offering, on behalf of Napoleon, to sell to the United States, not the Floridas at all, but merely Louisiana, "a raw little semi-tropical frontier town and an unexplored wilderness."

Suppose Livingston had rejected the offer? Or suppose Gadsden had not exceeded his instructions in Mexico and boldly grasped the opportunity that offered to rectify and make secure our Southwestern frontier? Would this generation judge that they had been equal to their opportunities or their duties?

The difficulties which at present discourage us are largely of our own creation. It is not for any of us to think of attempting to apportion the blame. The only thing we are sure of is that it was for no lack of authority that we hesitated and drifted till the Tagals were convinced we were afraid of them, and could be driven out before reinforcements arrived. That was the very thing our officers had warned us against,—the least sign of hesitation or uncertainty,—the very danger every European with knowledge of the situation had dinned in our ears. Everybody declared that difficulties were sure to grow on our hands in geometrical proportion to our delays; and it was perfectly known to the respective branches of our Government primarily concerned that while the delay went on it was in neglect of a duty we had voluntarily assumed.

For the American Commissioners, with due authority, distinctly offered to assume responsibility, pending the ratification of the treaty, for the protection of life and property and the preservation of order throughout the whole archipelago. The Spanish Commissioners, after consultation with their Government, refused this, but agreed that each Power should be charged, pending the ratification, with the maintenance of order in the places where it was established. The American assent to that left absolutely no question as to the diminished but still grave responsibility thus devolved.[8] That responsibility was avoided from the hour the treaty was signed till the hour when the Tagal chieftain, at the head of an army he had been deliberately gathering and organizing, took things in his own hand and made the attack he had so long threatened. Disorder, forced loans, impressment, confiscation, seizure of waterworks, contemptuous violations of our guard-lines, and even the practical siege of the city of Manila, had meantime been going on within gunshot of troops held there inactive by the Nation which had volunteered responsibility for order throughout the archipelago, and had been distinctly left with responsibility for order in the island on which it was established. If the bitterest enemy of the United States had sought to bring upon it in that quarter the greatest trouble in the shortest time, he could have devised for that end no policy more successful than the one we actually pursued. There may have been controlling reasons for it. An opposite course might perhaps have cost more elsewhere than it saved in Luzon. On that point the public cannot now form even an opinion. But as to the effect in Luzon there is no doubt; and because of it we have the right to ask a delay in judgment about results there until the present evil can be undone.

The Carnival of Captious Objection.

Meantime, in accordance with a well-known and probably unchangeable law of human nature, this is the carnival and very heyday of the objectors. The air is filled with their discouragement.

Some exclaim that Americans are incapable of colonizing or of managing colonies; that there is something in our national character or institutions that wholly disqualifies us for the work. Yet the most successful colonies in the whole world were the thirteen original colonies on our Atlantic coast; and the most successful colonists were our own grandfathers! Have the grandsons so degenerated that they are incapable of colonizing at all, or of managing colonies? Who says so? Is it any one with the glorious history of this continental colonization bred in his bone and leaping in his blood? Or is it some refugee from a foreign country he was discontented with, who now finds pleasure in disparaging the capacity of the new country he came to, while he has neither caught its spirit nor grasped the meaning of its history?

Some bewail the alleged fact that, at any rate, our system has little adaptability to the control of colonies or dependencies. Has our system been found weaker, then, than other forms of government, less adaptable to emergencies, and with people less fit to cope with them? Is the difficulty inherent, or is it possible that the emergency may show, as emergencies have shown before, that whatever task intelligence, energy, and courage can surmount the American people and their Government can rise to?

It is said the conditions in our new possessions are wholly different from any we have previously encountered. This is true; and there is little doubt the new circumstances will bring great modifications in methods. That is an excellent reason, among others, for some doubt at the outset as to whether we know all about it, but not for despairing of our capacity to learn. It might be remembered that we have encountered some varieties of conditions already. The work in Florida was different from that at Plymouth Rock; Louisiana and Texas showed again new sets of conditions; California others; Puget Sound and Alaska still others; and we did not always have unbroken success and plain sailing from the outset in any of them.

It is said we cannot colonize the tropics, because our people cannot labor there. Perhaps not, especially if they refuse to obey the prudent precautions which centuries of experience have enjoined upon others. But what, then, are we going to do with Porto Rico? How soon are our people going to flee from Arizona? And why is life impossible to Americans in Manila and Cebu and Iloilo, but attractive to the throngs of Europeans who have built up those cities? Can we mine all over the world, from South Africa to the Klondike, but not in Palawan? Can we grow tobacco in Cuba, but not in Cebu; or rice in Louisiana, but not in Luzon?

An alarm is raised that our laboring classes are endangered by competition with cheap tropical labor or its products. How? The interpretation of the Constitution which would permit that is the interpretation which has been repudiated in an unbroken line of decisions for over half a century. Only one possibility of danger to American labor exists in our new possessions—the lunacy, or worse, of the dreamers who want to prepare for the admission of some of them as States in the American Union. Till then we can make any law we like to prevent the immigration of their laborers, and any tariff we like to regulate the admission of their products.

It is said we are pursuing a fine method for restoring order, by prolonging the war we began for humanity in order to force liberty and justice on an unwilling people at the point of the bayonet. The sneer is cheap. How else have these blessings been generally diffused? How often in the history of the world has barbarism been replaced by civilization without bloodshed? How were our own liberty and justice established and diffused on this continent? Would the process have been less bloody if a part of our own people had noisily taken the side of the English, the Mexican, or the savage, and protested against "extreme measures"?

Some say a war to extend freedom in Cuba or elsewhere is right, and therefore a duty; but the war in the Philippines now is purely selfish, and therefore a crime. The premise is inaccurate; it is a war we are in duty bound to wage at any rate till order is restored—but let that pass. Suppose it to be merely a war in defense of our own just rights and interests. Since when did such a war become wrong? Is our national motto to be, "Quixotic on the one hand, Chinese on the other"?

How much better it would have been, say others, to mind our own business! No doubt; but if we were to begin crying over spilt milk in that way, the place to begin was where the milk was spilled—in the Congress that resolved upon war with Spain. Since that congressional action we have been minding what it made our own business quite diligently, and an essential part of our business now is the responsibility for our own past acts, whether in Havana or Manila.

Some say that since we began the war for humanity, we are disgraced by coming out of it with increased territory. Then a penalty must always be imposed upon a victorious nation for presuming to do a good act. The only nation to be exempt from such a penalty upon success is to be the nation that was in the wrong! It is to have a premium, whether successful or not; for it is thus relieved, even in defeat, from the penalty which modern practice in the interest of civilization requires—the payment of an indemnity for the cost of an unjust war. Furthermore, the representatives of the nation that does a good act are thus bound to reject any opportunity for lightening the national load it entails. They must leave the full burden upon their country, to be dealt with in due time by the individual taxpayer!

Again, we have superfine discussions of what the United States "stands for." It does not stand, we are told, for foreign conquest, or for colonies or dependencies, or other extensions of its power and influence. It stands solely for the development of the individual man. There is a germ of a great truth in this, but the development of the truth is lost sight of. Individual initiative is a good thing, and our institutions do develop it—and its consequences! There is a species of individualism, too, about a bulldog. When he takes hold he holds on. It may as well be noticed by the objectors that that is a characteristic much appreciated by American people. They, too, hold on. They remember, besides, a pregnant phrase of their fathers, who "ordained this Constitution," among other things, "to promote the general welfare." That is a thing for which "this Government stands" also; and woe to the public servant who rejects brilliant opportunities to promote it—on the Pacific Ocean no less than the Atlantic, by commerce no less than by agriculture or manufactures.

It is said the Philippines are worthless—have, in fact, already cost us more than the value of their entire trade for many years to come. So much the more, then, are we bound to do our duty by them. But we have also heard in turn, and from the same quarters, that every one of our previous acquisitions was worthless.

Again, it is said our continent is more than enough for all our needs, and our extensions should stop at the Pacific. What is this but proposing such a policy of self-sufficient isolation as we are accustomed to reprobate in China—planning now to develop only on the soil on which we stand, and expecting the rest of the world to protect our trade if we have any? Can a nation with safety set such limits to its development? When a tree stops growing, our foresters tell us, it is ripe for the ax. When a man stops in his physical and intellectual growth he begins to decay. When a business stops growing it is in danger of decline. When a nation stops growing it has passed the meridian of its course, and its shadows fall eastward.

Is China to be our model, or Great Britain? Or, better still, are we to follow the instincts of our own people? The policy of isolating ourselves is a policy for the refusal of both duties and opportunities—duties to foreign nations and to civilization, which cannot be respectably evaded; opportunities for the development of our power on the Pacific in the Twentieth Century, which it would be craven to abandon. There has been a curious "about face," an absolute reversal of attitude toward England, on the part of our Little Americans, especially at the East and among the more educated classes. But yesterday nearly all of them were pointing to England as a model. There young men of education and position felt it a duty to go into politics. There they had built up a model civil service. There their cities were better governed, their streets cleaner, their mails more promptly delivered. There the responsibilities of their colonial system had enforced the purification of domestic politics, the relentless punishment of corrupt practices, and the abolition of bribery in elections, either by money or by office. There they had foreign trade, and a commercial marine, and a trained and efficient foreign service, and to be an English citizen was to have a safeguard the whole world round. Our young men were commended to their example; our legislators were exhorted to study their practice and its results. Suddenly these same teachers turn around. They warn us against the infection of England's example. They tell us her colonial system is a failure; that she would be stronger without her colonies than with them; that she is eaten up with "militarism"; that to keep Cuba or the Philippines is what a selfish, conquering, land-grabbing, aristocratic government like England would do, and that her policy and methods are utterly incompatible with our institutions. When a court thus reverses itself without obvious reason (except a temporary partizan purpose), our people are apt to put their trust in other tribunals.

The Future.

"I had thought," said Wendell Phillips, in his noted apology for standing for the first time in his antislavery life under the flag of his country, and welcoming the tread of Massachusetts men marshaled for war—"I had thought Massachusetts wholly choked with cotton-dust and cankered with gold." If Little Americans have thought so of their country in these stirring days, and have fancied that initial reverses would induce it to abandon its duty, its rights, and its great permanent interests, they will live to see their mistake. They will find it giving a deaf ear to these unworthy complaints of temporary trouble or present loss, and turning gladly from all this incoherent and resultless clamor to the new world opening around us. Already it draws us out of ourselves. The provincial isolation is gone; and provincial habits of thought will go. There is a larger interest in what other lands have to show and teach; a larger confidence in our own; a higher resolve that it shall do its whole duty to mankind, moral as well as material, international as well as national, in such fashion as becomes time's latest offspring and its greatest. We are grown more nearly citizens of the world.

This new knowledge, these new duties and interests, must have two effects—they must extend our power, influence, and trade, and they must elevate the public service. Every returning soldier or traveler tells the same story—that the very name "American" has taken a new significance throughout the Orient. The shrewd Oriental no longer regards us as a second- or third-class Power. He has just seen the only signs he recognizes of a nation that knows its rights and dare maintain them—a nation that has come to stay, with an empire of its own in the China Sea, and a Navy which, from what he has seen, he believes will be able to defend it against the world. He straightway concludes, after the Oriental fashion, that it is a nation whose citizens must henceforth be secure in all their rights, whose missionaries must be endured with patience and even protected, and whose friendship must be sedulously cultivated. The national prestige is enormously increased, and trade follows prestige—especially in the farther East. Not within a century, not during our whole history, has such a field opened for our reaping. Planted directly in front of the Chinese colossus, on a great territory of our own, we have the first and best chance to profit by his awakening. Commanding both sides of the Pacific, and the available coal-supplies on each, we command the ocean that, according to the old prediction, is to bear the bulk of the world's commerce in the Twentieth Century. Our remote but glorious land between the Sierras and the sea may then become as busy a hive as New England itself, and the whole continent must take fresh life from the generous blood of this natural and necessary commerce between people of different climates and zones.

But these developments of power and trade are the least of the advantages we may hopefully expect. The faults in American character and life which the Little Americans tell us prove the people unfit for these duties are the very faults that will be cured by them. The recklessness and heedless self-sufficiency of youth must disappear. Great responsibilities, suddenly devolved, must sober and elevate now, as they have always done in natures not originally bad, throughout the whole history of the world.

The new interests abroad must compel an improved foreign service. It has heretofore been worse than we ever knew, and also better. On great occasions and in great fields our diplomatic record ranks with the best in the world. No nation stands higher in those new contributions to International Law which form the high-water mark of civilization from one generation to another. At the same time, in fields less under the public eye, our foreign service has been haphazard at the best, and often bad beyond belief—ludicrous and humiliating. The harm thus wrought to our national good name and the positive injury to our trade have been more than we realized. We cannot escape realizing them now, and when the American people wake up to a wrong they are apt to right it.

More important still should be the improvement in the general public service at home and in our new possessions. New duties must bring new methods. Ward politics were banished from India and Egypt as the price of successful administration, and they must be excluded from Porto Rico and Luzon. The practical common sense of the American people will soon see that any other course is disastrous. Gigantic business interests must come to reinforce the theorists in favor of a reform that shall really elevate and purify the Civil Service.

Hand in hand with these benefits to ourselves, which it is the duty of public servants to secure, go benefits to our new wards and benefits to mankind. There, then, is what the United States is to "stand for" in all the resplendent future: the rights and interests of its own Government; the general welfare of its own people; the extension of ordered liberty in the dark places of the earth; the spread of civilization and religion, and a consequent increase in the sum of human happiness in the world.

VIII

LATER ASPECTS OF OUR NEW DUTIES

This address was delivered on the invitation of the Board of Trustees, at Princeton University, in Alexander Hall, on October 21, 1899.

LATER ASPECTS OF OUR NEW DUTIES

The invitation for to-day with which Princeton honored me was accompanied with the hint that a discussion of some phase of current public affairs would not be unwelcome. That phase which has for the past year or two most absorbed public attention is now more absorbing than ever. Elsewhere I have already spoken upon it, more, perhaps, than enough. But I cannot better obey the summons of this honored and historic University, or better deserve the attention of this company of scholars, gentlemen, and patriots, than by saying with absolute candor what its present aspects prompt.

Questions that have been Disposed of.

And first, the chaos of opinion into which the country was thrown by the outbreak of the Spanish-American War ceases to be wholly without form and void. The discussions of a year have clarified ideas; and on some points we may consider that the American people have substantially reached definite conclusions.

There is no need, therefore, to debate laboriously before you whether Dewey was right in going to Manila. Everybody now realizes that, once war was begun, absolutely the most efficient means of making it speedily and overwhelmingly victorious, as well as of defending the most exposed half of our own coast, was to go to Manila. "Find the Spanish fleet and destroy it" was as wise an order as the President ever issued, and he was equally wise in choosing the man to carry it out.

So, also, there is no need to debate whether Dewey was right in staying there. From that come his most enduring laurels. The American people admire him for the battle which sank the Spanish navy; but they trust and love him for the months of trial and triumph that followed. The Administration that should have ordered him to abandon the Eastern foothold he had conquered for his country—to sail away like a sated pirate from the port where his victory broke down all civilized authority but our own, and his presence alone prevented domestic anarchy and foreign spoliation—would have deserved to be hooted out of the capital.

So, again, there is no need to debate whether the Peace Commissioners should have thrown away in Paris what Dewey had won in Manila. The public servant who, without instructions, should in a gush of irresponsible sentimentality abandon great possessions to which his country is justly entitled, whether by conquest or as indemnity for unjust war, would be not only an unprofitable but a faithless servant. It was their obvious duty to hold what Dewey had won, at least till the American people had time to consider and decide otherwise.

Is there any need to debate whether the American people will abandon it now? Those who have a fancy for that species of dialectics may weigh the chances, and evolve from circumstances of their own imagination, and canons of national and international obligation of their own manufacture, conclusions to their own liking. I need not consume much of your time in that unprofitable pursuit. We may as well, here and now, keep our feet on solid ground, and deal with facts as they are. The American people are in lawful possession of the Philippines, with the assent of all Christendom, with a title as indisputable as the title to California; and, though the debate will linger for a while, and perhaps drift unhappily into partizan contention, the generation is yet unborn that will see them abandoned to the possession of any other Power. The Nation that scatters principalities as a prodigal does his inheritance is too sentimental and moon-shiny for the Nineteenth Century or the Twentieth, and too unpractical for Americans of any period. It may flourish in Arcadia or Altruria, but it does not among the sons of the Pilgrims, or on the continent they subdued by stern struggle to the uses of civilization.

Nevertheless, our people did stop to consider very carefully their constitutional powers. I believe we have reached a point also where the result of that consideration may be safely assumed. The constitutional arguments have been fully presented and the expositions and decisions marshaled. It is enough now to say that the preponderance of constitutional authorities, with Gouverneur Morris, Daniel Webster, and Thomas H. Benton at their head, and the unbroken tendency of decisions by the courts of the United States for at least the last fifty years, from Mr. Chief Justice Waite and Mr. Justice Miller and Mr. Justice Stanley Matthews, of the Supreme Court, down to the very latest utterance on the subject, that of Mr. Justice Morrow of the Circuit Court of Appeals, sustain the power to acquire "territory or other property" anywhere, and govern it as we please.[9] Inhabitants of such territory (not obviously incapable) are secure in the civil rights guaranteed by the Constitution; but they have no political rights under it, save as Congress confers them. The evidence in support of this view has been fully set forth, examined, and weighed, and, unless I greatly mistake, a popular decision on the subject has been reached. The constitutional power is no longer seriously disputed, and even those who raised the doubt do not seem now to rely upon it.

Contributions to International Law and Morality.

In thus summarizing what has been already settled or disposed of in our dealings with the questions of the war, I may be permitted to pause for a moment on the American contributions it brought about to international morality and law. On the day on which the American Peace Commissioners to Paris sailed for home after the ceremonial courtesy with which their labors were concluded, the most authoritative journal in the world published an interview with the eminent President of the corresponding Spanish Commission, then and for some time afterward President also of the Spanish Senate, in which he was reported as saying: "We knew in advance that we should have to deal with an implacable conqueror, who would in no way concern himself with any pre-existing International Law, but whose sole object was to reap from victory the largest possible advantage. This conception of International Law is absolutely new; it is no longer a case of might against right, but of might without right.... The Americans have acted as vainqueurs parvenus."[10]

Much may be pardoned to the anguish of an old and trusted public servant over the misfortunes of his native land. We may even, in our sympathy, endeavor to forget what country it was that proposed to defy the agreements of the Conference of Paris and the general judgment of nations by resorting to privateering, or what country it was that preferred to risk becoming an asylum for the criminals of a continent rather than revive, even temporarily, that basic and elementary implement of modern international justice, an extradition treaty, which had been in force with acceptable results for over twenty years. But when Americans are stigmatized as "vainqueurs parvenus," who by virtue of mere strength violate International Law against a prostrate foe, and when one of the ablest of their American critics encourages the Spanish contention by talking of our "bulldog diplomacy at Paris," it gives us occasion to challenge the approval of the world—as the facts amply warrant—for the scrupulous conformity to existing International Law, and the important contributions to its beneficent advancement that have distinguished the action of the United States throughout these whole transactions. Having already set these forth in some detail before a foreign audience,[11] I must not now do more than offer the briefest summary.

The United States ended the toleration of Privateering. It was perfectly free to commission privateers on the day war was declared. Spain was equally free, and it was proclaimed from Madrid that the Atlantic would soon swarm with them, sweeping American commerce from the ocean. Under these circumstances one of the very first and noblest acts of the President was to announce that the United States would not avail itself of the right to send out privateers, reserved under the Declaration of Paris. The fast-thickening disasters of Spain prevented her from doing it, and thus substantially completed the practice or acquiescence of the civilized world, essential to the acceptance of a principle in International Law. It is safe to assume that Christendom will henceforth treat Privateering as under international ban.

The United States promoted the cause of genuine International Arbitration by promptly and emphatically rejecting an insidious proposal for a spurious one. It taught those who deliberately prefer War to Arbitration, and, when beaten at it, seek then to get the benefit of a second remedy, that honest Arbitration must come before War, to avert its horrors, not after War, to evade its penalties.

The United States promoted peace among nations, and so served humanity, by sternly enforcing the rule that they who bring on an unjust war must pay for it. For years the overwhelming tendency of its people had been against any territorial aggrandizement, even a peaceful one; but it unflinchingly exacted the easiest, if not the only, payment Spain could make for a war that cost us, at the lowest, from four to five hundred million dollars, by taking Porto Rico, Guam, and the Philippines. It requires some courage to describe this as either a violation of International Law, or a display of unprecedented severity by an implacable conqueror, in the very city and before the very generation that saw the Franco-Prussian War concluded, not merely by a partition of territory, but also by a cash payment of a thousand millions indemnity.

The United States promoted the peaceful liberalizing of oppressive rule over all subject peoples by making it more difficult to negotiate loans in the markets of the world to subdue their outbreaks. For it firmly rejected in the Cuban adjustments the immoral doctrine that an ill-treated and revolting colony, after gaining its freedom, must still submit to the extortion from it of the cost of the parent country's unsuccessful efforts to subdue it. We therefore left the so-called Cuban bonds on the hands of the Power that issued them, or of the reckless lenders who advanced the money. At the same time the United States strained a point elsewhere in the direction of protecting any legitimate debt, and of dealing generously with a fallen foe, by a payment which the most carping critic will some day be ashamed to describe as "buying the inhabitants of the Philippines at two dollars a head."[12]

All these are acts distinctly in accord with International Law so far as it exists and applies, and distinctly tending to promote its humane and Christian extension. Let me add, in a word, that the peace negotiations in no way compromised or affected the Monroe Doctrine, which stands as firm as ever, though much less important with the disappearance of any probable opposition to it; and that the prestige they brought smoothed the way for the one hopeful result of the Czar's Conference at The Hague, a response to the American proposal for a permanent International Court of Arbitration.

A trifling but characteristic inaccuracy concerning the Peace Commission may as well be corrected before the subject is left. This is the statement, apparently originating from Malay sources, but promptly indorsed in this country by unfriendly critics, to the effect that the representative of Aguinaldo was uncivilly refused a hearing in Paris. It was repeated, inadvertently, no doubt, with many other curious distortions of historic facts, only the other day, by a distinguished statesman in Chicago.[13] As he put it, the doors were slammed in their faces in Washington as well as in Paris. Now, whatever might have happened, the door was certainly never slammed in their faces in Paris, for they never came to it. On the contrary, every time Mr. Agoncillo approached any member of the Commission on the subject, he was courteously invited to send the Commissioners a written request for a hearing, which would, at any rate, receive immediate consideration. No such request ever came, and any Filipino who wrote for a hearing in Paris was heard.

The Present Duty.

Meanwhile we are now in the midst of hostilities with a part of the native population, originating in an unprovoked attack upon our troops in the city they had wrested from the Spaniards, before final action on the treaty. It is easy to say that we ought not to have got into this conflict, and to that I might agree. "I tell you, they can't put you in jail on that charge," said the learned and disputatious counsel to the client who had appealed from his cell for help. "But I *am* in," was the sufficient answer. The question just then was not what might have been done, but what can be done. I wish to urge that we can only end this conflict by manfully fighting through it. The talk one hears that the present situation calls for "diplomacy" seems to be mistimed. That species of diplomacy which consists in the tact of prompt action in the right line at the right time might, quite possibly, have prevented the present hostilities. Any diplomacy now would seem to our Tagal antagonists the raising of the white flag—the final proof that the American people do not sustain their Army in the face of unprovoked attack. Every witness who came before the American Peace Commission in Paris, or sent it a written statement, English, German, Belgian, Malay, or American, said the same thing. Absolutely the one essential for dealing with the Filipinos was to convince them at the very outset that what you began you stood to; that you did not begin without consideration of right and duty, or quail then before opposition; that your purpose was inexorable and your power irresistible, while submission to it would always insure justice. On the contrary, once let them suspect that protests would dissuade and turbulence deter you, and all the Oriental instinct for delay and bargaining for better terms is aroused, along with the special Malay genius for intrigue and double-dealing, their profound belief that every man has his price, and their childish ignorance as to the extent to which stump speeches here against any Administration can cause American armies beyond the seas to retreat.

No; the toast which Henry Clay once gave in honor of an early naval hero fits the present situation like a glove. He proposed "the policy which looks to peace as the end of war, and war as the means of peace." In that light I maintain that the conflict we are prosecuting is in the line of national necessity and duty; that we cannot turn back; that the truest humanity condemns needless delay or half-hearted action, and demands overwhelming forces and irresistible onset.

Eliminate Temporary Discouragements.

But in considering this duty, just as in estimating the Treaty of Paris, we have the right to eliminate all account of the trifling success, so far, in the Philippines, or of the great trouble and cost. What it was right to do there, and what we are bound to do now, must not be obscured by faults of hesitation or insufficient preparation, for which neither the Peace Commissioners nor the people are responsible. I had occasion to say before a college audience last June what I now repeat with the additional emphasis subsequent events have warranted—that the difficulties which at present discourage us are largely of our own making; and I repeat that it is still not for us, here and now, to apportion the blame. We have not the knowledge to say just who, or whether any man or body, is wholly at fault. What we do know is that the course of hesitation and inaction which the Nation pursued in face of an openly maturing attack was precisely the policy sure to give us the greatest trouble, and that we are now paying the penalty. If the opposite course had been taken at the outset—unless all the testimony from foreign observers and from our own officers is at fault—there would have been either no outbreak at all, or only one easily controlled and settled to the general satisfaction of most of the civilized and semi-civilized inhabitants of the island.

On the personal and partizan disputes already lamentably begun, as to senatorial responsibility, congressional responsibility, or the responsibility of this or that executive officer, we have no occasion here to enter. What we have a right to insist on is that our general policy in the Philippines shall not be shaped now merely by the just discontent with the bad start. The reports of continual victories, that roll back on us every week, like the stone of Sisyphus, and need to be won over again next week, the mistakes of a censorship that was absolutely right as a military measure, but may have been unintelligently, not to say childishly, conducted—all these are beside the real question. They must not obscure the duty of restoring order in the regions where our troops have been assailed, or prejudice our subsequent course.

I venture to say of that course that neither our duty nor our interest will permit us to stop short of a pacification which can only end in the establishment of such local self-government as the people are found capable of conducting, and its extension just as far and as fast as the people prove fit for it.

Pacification and Natural Course of Organization.

The natural development thus to be expected would probably proceed safely, along the lines of least resistance, about in this order: First, and till entirely clear that it is no longer needed, Military Government. Next, the rule of either Military or Civil Governors (for a considerable time probably the former), relying gradually more and more on native agencies. Thirdly, the development of Dependencies, with an American Civil Governor, with their foreign relations and their highest courts controlled by us, and their financial system largely managed by members of a rigidly organized and jealously protected American Civil Service, but in most other respects steadily becoming more self-governing. And, finally, autonomous governments, looking to us for little save control of their foreign relations, profiting by the stability and order the backing of a powerful nation guarantees, cultivating more and more intimate trade and personal relations with that nation, and coming to feel themselves participants of its fortunes and renown.

Such a course Congress, after full investigation and deliberation, might perhaps wisely formulate. Such a course, with slight modifications to meet existing limitations as to his powers, has already been entered upon by the President, and can doubtless be carried on indefinitely by him until Congress acts. This action should certainly not be precipitate. The system demands most careful study, not only in the light of what the English and Dutch, the most successful holders of tropical countries, have done, but also in the light of the peculiar and varied circumstances that confront us on these different and distant islands, and among these widely differing races—circumstances to which no previous experience exactly applies, and for which no uniform system could be applicable. If Congress should take as long a time before action to study the problem as it has taken in the Sandwich Islands, or even in Alaska, the President's power would still be equal to the emergency, and the policy, while flexible, could still be made as continuous, coherent, and practical as his best information and ability would permit.

Evasions of Duty.

Against such a conscientious and painstaking course in dealing with the grave responsibilities that are upon us in the East, two lines of evasion are sure to threaten. The one is the policy of the upright but short-sighted and strictly continental patriot—the same which an illustrious statesman of another country followed in the Sudan: "Scuttle as quick as you can."

The other is the policy of the exuberant patriot who believes in the universal adaptability and immediate extension of American institutions. He thinks all men everywhere as fit to vote as himself, and wants them for partners. He is eager to have them prepare at once, in our new possessions, first in the West Indies, then in the East, to send Senators and Representatives to Congress, and his policy is: "Make Territories of them now, and States in the American Union as soon as possible." I wish to speak with the utmost respect of the sincere advocates of both theories, but must say that the one seems to me to fall short of a proper regard for either our duty or our interest, and the other to be national suicide.

Gentlemen in whose ability and patriotism we all have confidence have lately put the first of these policies for evading our duty in the form of a protest "against the expansion and establishment of the dominion of the United States, by conquest or otherwise, over unwilling peoples in any part of the globe." Of this it may be said, first, that any application of it to the Philippines probably assumes a factional and temporary outbreak to represent a settled unwillingness. New Orleans was as "unwilling," when Mr. Jefferson annexed it, as Aguinaldo has made Manila; and Aaron Burr came near making the whole Louisiana Territory far worse. Mr. Lincoln, you remember, always believed the people of North Carolina not unwilling to remain in the Union, yet we know what they did. But next, this protest contemplates evading the present responsibility by a reversal of our settled policy any way. Mr. Lincoln probably never doubted the unwillingness of South Carolina to remain in the Union, but that did not change his course. Mr. Seward never inquired whether the Alaskans were unwilling or not. The historic position of the United States, from the day when Jefferson braved the envenomed anti-expansion sentiment of his time and bought the territory west of the Mississippi, on down, has been to consider, not the willingness or unwillingness of any inhabitants, whether aboriginal or colonists, but solely our national opportunity, our own duty, and our own interests.

Is it said that this is Imperialism? That implies usurpation of power, and there is absolutely no ground for such a charge against this Administration at any one stage in these whole transactions. If any complaint here is to lie, it must relate to the critical period when we were accepting responsibility for order at Manila, and must be for the exercise of too little power, not too much. It is not Imperialism to take up honestly the responsibility for order we incurred before the world, and continue under it, even if that should lead us to extend the civil rights of the American Constitution over new regions and strange peoples. It is not Imperialism when duty keeps us among these chaotic, warring, distracted tribes, civilized, semi-civilized, and barbarous, to help them, as far as their several capacities will permit, toward self-government, on the basis of those civil rights.

A terser and more taking statement of opposition has been recently attributed to a gentleman highly honored by this University and by his townsmen here. I gladly seize this opportunity, as a consistent opponent during his whole political life, to add that his words carry great weight throughout the country by reason of the unquestioned ability, courage, and patriotic devotion he has brought to the public service. He is reported as protesting simply against "the use of power in the extension of American institutions." But does not this, if applied to the present situation, seem also to miss an important distinction? What planted us in the Philippines was the use of our power in the most efficient naval and military defense then available for our own institutions where they already exist, against the attack of Spain. If the responsibility entailed by the result of these acts in our own defense does involve some extension of our institutions, shall we therefore run away from it? If a guaranty to chaotic tribes of the civil rights secured by the American Constitution does prove to be an incident springing from the discharge of the duty that has rested upon us from the moment we drove Spain out, is that a result so objectionable as to warrant us in abandoning our duty?

There is, it is true, one other alternative—the one which Aguinaldo himself is said to have suggested, and which has certainly been put forth in his behalf with the utmost simplicity and sincerity by a conspicuous statesman at Chicago. We might at once solicit peace from Aguinaldo. We might then encourage him to extend his rule over the whole country,—Catholic, pagan, and Mohammedan, willing and unwilling alike,—and promise him whatever aid might be necessary for that task. Meantime, we should undertake to protect him against outside interference from any European or Asiatic nation whose interests on that oceanic highway and in those commercial capitals might be imperiled![14] I do not desire to discuss that proposition. And I submit to candid men that there are just those three courses, and no more, now open to us—to run away, to protect Aguinaldo, or to back up our own army and firmly hold on!

Objections to Duty.

If this fact be clearly perceived, if the choice between these three courses be once recognized as the only choice the present situation permits, our minds will be less disturbed by the confused cries of perplexity and discontent that still fill the air. Thus men often say, "If you believe in liberty for yourself, why refuse it to the Tagals?" That is right; they should have, in the degree of their capacity, the only kind of liberty worth having in the world, the only kind that is not a curse to its possessors and to all in contact with them—ordered liberty, under law, for which the wisdom of man has not yet found a better safeguard than the guaranties of civil rights in the Constitution of the United States. Who supposes that to be the liberty for which Aguinaldo is fighting? What his people want, and what the statesman at Chicago wishes us to use the Army and Navy of the United States to help him get, is the liberty to rule others—the liberty first to turn our own troops out of the city and harbor we had in our own self-defense captured from their enemies; the liberty next to rule that great commercial city, and the tribes of the interior, instead of leaving us to exercise the rule over them that events have forced upon us, till it is fairly shown that they can rule themselves.

Again it is said, "You are depriving them of freedom." But they never had freedom, and could not have it now. Even if they could subdue the other tribes in Luzon, they could not establish such order on the other islands and in the waters of the archipelago as to deprive foreign Powers of an immediate excuse for interference. What we are doing is in the double line of preventing otherwise inevitable foreign seizure and putting a stop to domestic war.

"But you cannot fit people for freedom. They must fit themselves, just as we must do our own crawling and stumbling in order to learn to walk." The illustration is unfortunate. Must the crawling baby, then, be abandoned by its natural or accidental guardian, and left to itself to grow strong by struggling, or to perish, as may happen? Must we turn the Tagals loose on the foreigners in Manila, and on their enemies in the other tribes, that by following their instincts they may fit themselves for freedom?

Again, "It will injure us to exert power over an unwilling people, just as slavery injured the slaveholders themselves." Then a community is injured by maintaining a police. Then a court is injured by rendering a just decree, and an officer by executing it. Then it is a greater injury, for instance, to stop piracy than to suffer from it.

Then the manly exercise of a just responsibility enfeebles instead of developing and strengthening a nation.

"Governments derive their just powers from the consent of the governed." "No man is good enough to govern another against his will." Great truths, from men whose greatness and moral elevation the world admires. But there is a higher authority than Jefferson or Lincoln, Who said: "If a man smite thee on thy right cheek, turn to him the other also." Yet he who acted literally on even that divine injunction toward the Malays that attacked our Army in Manila would be a congenital idiot to begin with, and his corpse, while it lasted, would remain an object-lesson of how not to deal with the present stage of Malay civilization and Christianity.

Why mourn over our present course as a departure from the policy of the fathers? For a hundred years the uniform policy which they began and their sons continued has been acquisition, expansion, annexation, reaching out to remote wildernesses far more distant and inaccessible then than the Philippines are now—to disconnected regions like Alaska, to island regions like Midway, the Guano Islands, the Aleutians, the Sandwich Islands, and even to quasi-protectorates like Liberia and Samoa. Why mourn because of the precedent we are establishing? The precedent was established before we were born. Why distress ourselves with the thought that this is only the beginning, that it opens the door to unlimited expansion? The door is wide open now, and has been ever since Livingston in Paris jumped at Talleyrand's offer to sell him the wilderness west of the Mississippi instead of the settlements eastward to Florida, which we had been trying to get; and Jefferson eagerly sustained him. For the rest, the task that is laid upon us now is not proving so easy as to warrant this fear that we shall soon be seeking unlimited repetitions of it.

Evasion by Embrace.

That danger, in fact, can come only if we shirk our present duty by the second of the two alternative methods of evasion I have mentioned—the one favored by the exuberant patriot who wants to clasp Cuban, Kanaka, and Tagal alike to his bosom as equal partners with ourselves in our inheritance from the fathers, and take them all into the Union as States.

We will be wise to open our eyes at once to the gravity and the insidious character of this danger—the very worst that could threaten the American Union. Once begun, the rivalry of parties and the fears of politicians would insure its continuance. With Idaho and Wyoming admitted, they did not dare prolong the exclusion even of Utah, and so we have the shame of seeing an avowed polygamist with a prima facie right to sit in our Congress as a legislator not merely for Utah, but for the whole Union. At this moment scarcely a politician dares frankly avow unalterable opposition to the admission of Cuba, if she should seek it. Yet, bad as that would be, it would necessarily lead to worse. Others in the West Indies might not linger long behind. In any event, with Cuba a State, Porto Rico could not be kept a Territory. No more could the Sandwich Islands. And then, looming direct in our path, like a volcano rising out of the mist on the affrighted vision of mariners tempest-tossed in tropic seas, is the specter of such States as Luzon and the Visayas and Haiti.

They would have precedents, too, to quote, and dangerous ones. When we bought Louisiana we stipulated in the treaty that "the inhabitants of the ceded territory shall be incorporated in the Union of the United States and admitted as soon as possible, according to the principles of the Federal Constitution, to the enjoyment of all the rights, advantages, and immunities of citizens of the United States." We made almost identically the same stipulation when we bought Florida. When one of the most respected in the long line of our able Secretaries of State, Mr. William L. Marcy, negotiated a treaty in 1854 for the annexation of the Sandwich Islands, he provided that they should be incorporated as a State, with the same degree of sovereignty as other States, and on perfect equality with them. The schemes prior to 1861 for the purchase or annexation of Cuba practically all looked to the same result. Not till the annexation of San Domingo was proposed did this feature disappear from our treaties. It is only candid to add that the habit of regarding this as the necessary destiny of any United States Territory as soon as it has sufficient population has been universal. It is no modern vagary, but the practice, if not the theory, of our whole national life, that would open the doors of our Senate and House, and give a share in the

Government to these wild-eyed newcomers from the islands of the sea.

The calamity of admitting them cannot be overrated. Even in the case of the best of these islands, it would demoralize and degrade the national suffrage almost incalculably below the point already reached. To the Senate, unwieldy now, and greatly changed in character from the body contemplated by the Constitution, it would be disastrous. For the present States of the Union it would be an act of folly like that of a business firm which blindly steered for bankruptcy by freely admitting to full partnership new members, strangers, and non-residents, not only otherwise ill qualified, but with absolutely conflicting interests. And it would be a distinct violation of the clause in the preamble that "we, the people,... do ordain and establish this Constitution for the United States of *America*."

There is the only safe ground—on the letter and the spirit of the Constitution. It contemplated a Continental Union of sovereign States. It limited that Union to the American Continent. The man that takes it farther sounds its death-knell.

The General Welfare.

I have designedly left to the last any estimate of the material interests we serve by holding on in our present course. Whatever these may be, they are only a subordinate consideration. We are in the Philippines, as we are in the West Indies, because duty sent us; and we shall remain because we have no right to run away from our duty, even if it does involve far more trouble than we foresaw when we plunged into the war that entailed it. The call to duty, when once plainly understood, is a call Americans never fail to answer, while to calls of interest they have often shown themselves incredulous or contemptuous.

But the Constitution we revere was also ordained "to promote the general welfare," and he is untrue to its purpose who squanders opportunities. Never before have they been showered upon us in such bewildering profusion. Are the American people to rise to the occasion? Are they to be as great as their country? Or shall the historian record that at this unexampled crisis they were controlled by timid ideas and short-sighted views, and so proved unequal to the duty and the opportunity which unforeseen circumstances brought to their doors? The two richest archipelagos in the world are practically at our disposal. The greatest ocean on the globe has been put in our hands, the ocean that is to bear the commerce of the Twentieth Century. In the face of this prospect, shall we prefer, with the teeming population that century is to bring us, to remain a "hibernating nation, living off its own fat—a hermit nation," as Mr. Senator Davis has asked? For our first Assistant Secretary of State, Mr. Hill, was right when he said that not to enter the Open Door in Asia means the perpetual isolation of this continent.

Have they any Value?

Are we to be discouraged by the cry that the new possessions are worthless? Not while we remember how often and under what circumstances we have heard that cry before. Half the public men of the period denounced Louisiana as worthless. Eminent statesmen made merry in Congress over the idea that Oregon or Washington could be of any use. Daniel Webster, in the most solemn and authoritative tones Massachusetts has ever employed, assured his fellow-Senators that, in his judgment, California was not worth a dollar.

Is it said that the commercial opportunities in the Orient, or at least in the Philippines, are overrated? So it used to be said of the Sandwich Islands. But what does our experience show? Before their annexation even, but after we had taken this little archipelago under our protection and into our commercial system, our ocean tonnage in that trade became nearly double as heavy as with Great Britain. Why? Because, while we have lost the trade of the Atlantic, superior advantages make the Pacific ours. Is it said that elsewhere on the Pacific we can do as well without a controlling political influence as with it? Look again! Mexico buys our products at the rate of $1.95 for each inhabitant; South America at the rate of 90 cents; Great Britain at the rate of $13.42; Canada at the rate of $14; and the Hawaiian Islands at the rate of $53.35 for each inhabitant. Look at the trade of the chief city on the Pacific coast. All Mexico and Central America, all the western parts of South America and of Canada, are as near to it as is Honolulu; and comparison of the little Sandwich Islands in population with any of them would be ridiculous. Yet none of them bought as much salmon in San Francisco as Hawaii, and no countries bought more save England and Australia. No countries bought as much barley, excepting Central America; and even in the staff of life, the California flour, which all the world buys, only five countries outranked Hawaii in purchases in San Francisco.

No doubt a part of this result is due to the nearness of Hawaii to our markets, and her distance from any others capable of competing with us, and another part to a favorable system of reciprocity. Nevertheless, nobody doubts the advantage our dealers have derived in the promotion of trade from controlling political relations and frequent intercourse. There are those who deny that "trade follows the flag," but even they admit that it leaves if the flag does. And, independent of these advantages, and reckoning by mere distance, we still have the better of any European rivals in the Philippines. Now, assume that the Filipino would have far fewer wants than the Kanaka or his coolie laborer, and would do far less work for the means to gratify them. Admit, too, that, with the Open Door, our political relations and frequent intercourse could have barely a fifth or a sixth of the effect there they have had in the Sandwich Islands. Roughly cast up even that result, and say whether it is a value which the United States should throw away as not worth considering!

And the greatest remains behind. For the trade in the Philippines will be but a drop in the bucket compared to that of China, for which they give us an unapproachable foothold. But let it never be forgotten that the confidence of Orientals goes only to those whom they recognize as strong enough and determined enough always to hold their own and protect their rights! The worst possible introduction for the Asiatic trade would be an irresolute abandonment of our foothold because it was too much trouble to keep, or because some Malay and half-breed insurgents said they wanted us away.

The Future.

Have you considered for whom we hold these advantages in trust? They belong not merely to the seventy-five millions now within our borders, but to all who are to extend the fortunes and preserve the virtues of the Republic in the coming century. Their numbers cannot increase in the startling ratio this century has shown. If they did the population of the United States a hundred years hence would be over twelve hundred millions. That ratio is impossible, but nobody gives reasons why we should not increase half as fast. Suppose we do actually increase only one fourth as fast in the Twentieth Century as in the Nineteenth. To what height would not the three hundred millions of Americans whom even that ratio foretells bear up the seething industrial activities of the continent! To what corner of the world would they not need to carry their commerce? What demands on tropical productions would they not make? What outlets for their adventurous youth would they not require? With such a prospect before us, who thinks that we should shrink from an enlargement of our national sphere because of the limitations that bound, or the dangers that threatened, before railroads, before ocean steamers, before telegraphs and ocean cables, before the enormous development of our manufactures, and the training of executive and organizing faculties in our people on a constantly increasing scale for generations?

Does the prospect alarm? Is it said that our Nation is already too great, that all its magnificent growth only adds to the conflicting interests that must eventually tear it asunder? What cement, then, like that of a great common interest beyond our borders, that touches not merely the conscience but the pocket and the pride of all alike, and marshals us in the face of the world, standing for our own?

What, then, is the conclusion of the whole matter? Hold fast! Stand firm in the place where Providence has put you, and do the duty a just responsibility for your own past acts imposes. Support the army you sent there. Stop wasting valuable strength by showing how things might be different if something different had been done a year and a half ago. Use the educated thought of the country for shaping best its course now, instead of chiefly finding fault with its history. Bring the best hope of the future, the colleges and the generation they are training, to exert the greatest influence and accomplish the most good by working intelligently in line with the patriotic aspirations and the inevitable tendencies of the American people, rather than against them. Unite the efforts of all men of good will to make the appointment of any person to these new and strange duties beyond seas impossible save for proved fitness, and his removal impossible save for cause. Rally the colleges and the churches, and all they influence, the brain and the conscience of the country, in a combined and irresistible demand for a genuine, trained, and pure Civil Service in our new possessions, that shall put to shame our detractors, and show to the world the Americans of this generation, equal still to the work of civilization and colonization, and leading the development of the coming century as bravely as their fathers led it in the last.

IX

A CONTINENTAL UNION

This speech was delivered on the invitation of the Massachusetts Club, at their regular dinner in Boston, March 3, 1900.

A CONTINENTAL UNION

A third of a century ago I had the honor to be a guest at this club, which met then, as now, in Young's Hotel. It has ever since been a pleasure to recall the men of Boston who gathered about the board, interested, as now, in the affairs of the Republic to which they were at once ornament and defense. Frank Bird sat at the head. Near him was Henry Wilson. John M. Forbes was here, and John A. Andrew, and George S. Boutwell, and George L. Stearns, and many another, eager in those times of trial to seek and know the best thing to be done to serve this country of our pride and love. They were practical business men, true Yankees in the best sense; and they spent no time then in quarreling over how we got into our trouble. Their one concern was how to get out to the greatest advantage of the country.

Honored now by another opportunity to meet with the club, I can do no better than profit by this example of your earlier days. You have asked me to speak on some phase of the Philippine question. I would like to concentrate your attention upon the present and practical phase, and to withdraw it for the time from things that are past and cannot be changed.

Things that Cannot be Undone.

Stare decisis. There are some things settled. Have we not a better and more urgent use for our time now than in showing why some of us would have liked them settled differently? In my State there is a dictum by an eminent judge of the Court of Appeals, so familiar now as to be a commonplace, to the effect that when that court has rendered its decision, there are only two things left to the disappointed advocate. One is to accept the result attained, and go to work on it as best he can; the other, to go down to the tavern and "cuss" the court. I want to suggest to those who dislike the past of the Philippine question that there is more important work pressing upon you at this moment than to cuss the court. You cannot change the past, but you may prevent some threatened sequences which even in your eyes would be far greater calamities.

There is no use bewailing the war with Spain. Nothing can undo it, and its results are upon us. There is no use arguing that Dewey should have abandoned his conquest. He didn't. There is no use regretting the Peace of Paris. For good or for ill, it is a part of the supreme law of the land. There is no use begrudging the twenty millions. They are paid. There is no use depreciating the islands, East or West. They are the property of the United States by an immutable title which, whatever some of our own people say, the whole civilized world recognizes and respects. There is no use talking about getting rid of them—giving them back to Spain, or turning them over to Aguinaldo, or simply running away from them. Whoever thinks that any one of these things could be done, or is still open to profitable debate, takes his observations—will you pardon me the liberty of saying it?—takes his observations too closely within the horizon of Boston Bay to know the American people.

They have not been persuaded and they cannot be persuaded that this is an inferior Government, incapable of any duty Providence (through the acts of a wicked Administration, if you choose) may send its way—duties which other nations could discharge, but we cannot. They do not and will not believe that it was any such maimed, imperfect, misshapen cripple from birth for which our forefathers made a place in the family of nations. Nor are they misled by the cry that, in a populous region, thronged by the ships and traders of all countries, where their own prosecution of a just war broke down whatever guaranties for order had previously existed, they are violating the natural rights of man by enforcing order. Just as little are they misled by the other cry that they are violating the right of self-government, and the Declaration of Independence, and the Constitution of the United States by preparing for the distracted, warring tribes of that region such local government as they may be found capable of conducting, in their various stages of development from pure barbarism toward civilization. The American people know they are thus proceeding to do just what Jefferson did in the vast region he bought from France—without the consent, by the way, either of its sovereign or its inhabitants. They know they are following in the exact path of all the constructive statesmen of the

Republic, from the days of the man who wrote the Declaration, and of those who made the Constitution, down to the days of the men who conquered California, bought Alaska, and denied the right of self-government to Jefferson Davis. They simply do not believe that a new light has been given to Mr. Bryan, or to the better men who are aiding him, greater and purer than was given to Washington, or to Jefferson, or to Lincoln.

And so I venture to repeat, without qualification or reserve, that what is past cannot be changed. Candid and dispassionate minds, knowing the American people of all political shades and in all sections of the country, can see no possibility that any party in power, whether the present one or its opponent, would or could, now or soon, if ever, abandon or give back one foot of the territory gained in the late war, and ours now by the supreme law of the land and with the assent of the civilized world. As well may you look to see California, which your own Daniel Webster, quite in a certain modern Massachusetts style, once declared in the Senate to be not worth a dollar, now abandoned to Mexico.

No Abstractions or Apologies or Attacks.

It seems to me, then, idle to thresh over old straw when the grain is not only winnowed, but gone to the mill. And so I am not here to discuss abstract questions: as, for example, whether in the year 1898 the United States was wise in going to war with Spain, though on that I might not greatly disagree with the malcontents; or as to the wisdom of expansion; or as to the possibility of a republic's maintaining its authority over a people without their consent. Nor am I here to apologize for my part in making the nation that was in the wrong and beaten in the late war pay for it in territory. I have never thought of denying or evading my own full share of responsibility in that matter. Conscious of a duty done, I am happily independent enough to be measurably indifferent as to a mere present and temporary effect. Whatever the verdict of the men of Massachusetts today, I contentedly await the verdict of their sons.

But, on the other hand, I am not here either to launch charges of treason against any opponent of these policies, who nevertheless loves the institutions founded on these shores by your ancestors, and wishes to perpetuate what they created. Least of all would it occur to me to utter a word in disparagement of your senior Senator, of whom it may be said with respectful and almost affectionate regard that he bears a warrant as authentic as that of the most distinguished of his predecessors to speak for the conscience and the culture of Massachusetts. Nor shall any reproach be uttered by me against another eminent son of the commonwealth and servant of the Republic, who was expected, as one of the officers of your club told me, to make this occasion distinguished by his presence. He has been represented as resenting the unchangeable past so sternly that he now hopes to aid in defeating the party he has helped to lead through former trials to present glory. If so, and if from the young and unremembering reproach should come, be it ours, silent and walking backward, merely to cast over him the mantle of his own honored service.

Common Duty and a Common Danger.

No, no! Let us have a truce to profitless disputes about what cannot be reversed. Censure us if you must. Even strike at your old associates and your own party if you will and when you can, without harming causes you hold dear. But for the duty of this hour, consider if there is not a common meeting-ground and instant necessity for union in a rational effort to avert present perils. This, then, is my appeal. Disagree as we may about the past, let us to-day at least see straight—see things as they are. Let us suspend disputes about what is done and cannot be undone, long enough to rally all the forces of good will, all the undoubted courage and zeal and patriotism that are now at odds, in a devoted effort to meet the greater dangers that are upon us.

For the enemy is at the gates. More than that, there is some reason to fear that, through dissensions from within, he may gain the citadel. In their eagerness to embarrass the advocates of what has been done, and with the vain hope of in some way undoing it, and so lifting this Nation of seventy-five millions bodily backward two years on its path, there are many who are still putting forth all their energies in straining our Constitution and defying our history, to show that we have no possessions whose people are not entitled to citizenship and ultimately to Statehood. Grant that, and instead of reversing engines safely in mid-career, as they vainly hope, they must simply plunge us over the precipice. The movement began in the demand that our Dingley tariff—as a matter of right, not of policy, for most of these people denounce the tariff itself as barbarous—that our Dingley tariff should of necessity be extended over Porto Rico as an integral part of the United States. Following an assent to this must have come inevitably all the other rights and privileges belonging to citizenship, and then no power could prevent the admission of the State of Porto Rico.

Some may think that in itself would be no great thing, though it is for you to say how Massachusetts would relish having this mixed population, a little more than half colonial Spanish, the rest negro and half-breed, illiterate, alien in language, alien in ideas of right, interests, and government, send in from the mid-Atlantic, nearly a third of the way over to Africa, two Senators to balance the votes of Mr. Hoar and Mr. Lodge; for you to say how Massachusetts would regard the spectacle of her senatorial vote nullified, and one third of her representation in the House offset on questions, for instance, of sectional and purely Northern interest, in the government of this continent, and in the administration of this precious heritage of our fathers.

Or, suppose Massachusetts to be so little Yankee (in the best sense still) that she could bear all this without murmur or objection—is it to be imagined that she can lift other States in this generation to her altruistic level? How would Kansas, for example, enjoy being balanced in the Senate, and nearly balanced in the House, on questions relating to the irrigation of her arid plains, or the protection of her beet-root industry, or on any others affecting the great central regions of this continent, by these voices from the watery waste of the ocean? Or how would West Virginia or Oregon or Connecticut, or half a dozen others of similar population, regard it to be actually outvoted in their own home, on their own continent, by this Spanish and negro waif from the mid-Atlantic?

All this, in itself, may seem to some unimportant, negligible, even trivial. At any rate, it would be inevitable; since no one is wild enough to believe that Porto Rico can be turned back to Spain, or bartered away, or abandoned by the generation that took it. But make its people citizens now, and you have already made it, potentially, a State. Then behind Porto Rico stands Cuba, and behind Cuba, in time, stand the whole of the West Indies, on whom that law of political gravitation which John Quincy Adams described will be perpetually acting with redoubled force. And behind them—no, far ahead of them, abreast of Porto Rico itself—stand the Philippines! The Constitution which our fathers reverently ordained for the United States of *America* is thus tortured by its professed friends into a crazy-quilt, under whose dirty folds must huddle the United States of America, of the West Indies, of the East Indies, and of Polynesia; and Pandemonium is upon us.

The Degradation of the Republic.

I implore you, as thinking men, pause long enough to realize the degradation of the Republic thus calmly contemplated by those who proclaim this to be our constitutional duty toward our possessions. The republican institutions I have been trained to believe in were institutions founded, like those of New England, on the Church and the school-house. They constitute a system only likely to endure among a people of high virtue and high intelligence. The republican government built up on this continent, while the most successful in the history of the world, is also the most complicated, the most expensive, and often the slowest. Such are its complications and checks and balances and interdependencies, which tax the intelligence, the patience, and the virtue of the highest Caucasian development, that it is a system absolutely unworkable by a group of Oriental and tropical races, more or less hostile to each other, whose highest type is a Chinese and Malay half-breed, and among whom millions, a majority possibly, are far below the level of the pure Malay.

What holds a nation together, unless it be community of interests, character, and language, and contiguous territory? What would more thoroughly insure its speedily flying to pieces than the lack of every one of these requisites? Over and over, the clearest-eyed students of history have predicted our own downfall even as a continental republic, in spite of our measurable enjoyment of all of them. How near we all believed we came to it once or twice! How manifestly, under the incongruous hodge-podge of additions to the Union thus proposed, we should be organizing with Satanic skill the exact conditions which have invariably led to such downfalls elsewhere!

Before the advent of the United States, the history of the world's efforts at republicanism was a monotonous record of failure. Your very school-boys are taught the reason. It was because the average of intelligence and morality was too low; because they lacked the self-restrained, self-governing quality developed in the Anglo-Saxon bone and fiber through all the centuries since Runnymede; because they grew unwieldy and lost cohesion by reason of unrelated territory, alien races and languages, and inevitable territorial and climatic conflicts of interest.

On questions vitally affecting the welfare of this continent it is inconceivable, unthinkable, that even altruistic Massachusetts should tolerate having her two Senators and thirteen Representatives neutralized by as many from Mindanao. Yet Mindanao has a greater population than Massachusetts, and its Mohammedan Malays are as keen for the conduct of public affairs, can talk as much, and look as shrewdly for the profit of it.

There are cheerful, happy-go-lucky public men who assure us that the national digestion has been proved equal to anything. Has it? Are we content, for example, with the way we have dealt with the negro problem in the Southern States? Do we think the suffrage question there is now on a permanent basis which either we or our Southern friends can be proud of, while we lack the courage either honestly to enforce the rule of the majority, or honestly to sanction a limitation of suffrage within lines of intelligence and thrift? How well would our famous national digestion probably advance if we filled up our Senate with twelve or fourteen more Senators, representing conditions incomparably worse?

Is it said this danger is imaginary? At this moment some of the purest and most patriotic men in Massachusetts, along with a great many of the very worst in the whole country, are vehemently declaring that our new possessions are already a part of the United States; that in spite of the treaty which reserved the question of citizenship and political status for Congress, their people are already citizens of the United States; and that no part of the United States can be arbitrarily and permanently excluded from Statehood.

The immediate contention, to be sure, is only about Porto Rico, and it is only a very little island. But who believes he can stop the avalanche? What wise man, at least, will take the risk of starting it? Who imagines that we can take in Porto Rico and keep out nearer islands when they come? Powerful elements are already pushing Cuba. Practically everybody recognizes now that we must retain control of Cuba's foreign relations. But beyond that, the same influences that came so near hurrying us into a recognition of the Cuban Republic and the Cuban debt are now sure that Cuba will very shortly be so "Americanized" (that is, overrun with American speculators) that it cannot be denied admission—that, in fact, it will be as American as Florida! And, after Cuba, the deluge! Who fancies that we could then keep San Domingo and Haiti out, or any West India island that applied, or our friends the Kanakas? Or who fancies that after the baser sort have once tasted blood, in the form of such rotten-borough States, and have learned to form their larger combinations with them, we shall still be able to admit as a matter of right a part of the territory exacted from Spain, and yet deny admission as a matter of right to the rest?

The Nation has lately been renewing its affectionate memories of a man who died in his effort to hold on, with or without their consent, to the States we already have on this continent, but who never dreamed of casting a drag-net over the world's archipelagos for more. Do we remember his birthday and forget his words? "This Government"—meaning that under the Constitution ordained for the United States of *America*—"this Government cannot permanently endure, half slave, half free." Who disputes it now? Well, then, can it endure half civilized and enlightened, half barbarous and pagan; half white, half black, brown, yellow, and mixed; half Northern and Western, half tropical and Oriental; one half a homogeneous continent, the rest in myriads of islands scattered half-way around the globe, but all eager to participate in ruling this continent which our fathers with fire and sword redeemed from barbarism and subdued to the uses of the highest civilization?

Clamor that Need not Disturb.

I will not insult your intelligence or your patriotism by imagining it possible that in view of such considerations you could consent to the madman's policy of taking these islands we control into full partnership with the States of this Union. Nor need you be much disturbed by the interested outcries as to the injustice you do by refusing to admit them.

When it is said you are denying the natural rights Mr. Jefferson proclaimed, you can answer that you are giving these people, in their distant islands, the identical form of government Mr. Jefferson himself gave to the territories on this continent which he bought. When it is said you are denying our own cardinal doctrine of self-government, you can point to the arrangements for establishing every particle of self-government with which these widely different tribes can be safely trusted, consistently with your responsibility for the preservation of order and the protection of life and property in that archipelago, and the pledge of more the moment they are found capable of it. When you are asked, as a leading champion[15] asked the other night at Philadelphia, "Does your liberation of one people give you the right to subjugate another?" you can answer him, "No; nor to allow and aid Aguinaldo to subjugate them, either, as you proposed." When the idle quibble that after Dewey's victory Spain had no sovereignty to cede is repeated, it may be asked, "Why acknowledge, then, that she did cede it in Porto Rico and relinquish it in Cuba, yet deny that she could cede it in the Philippines?" Finally, when they tell you in mock heroics, appropriated from the great days of the anti-slavery struggle for the cause now of a pinchbeck Washington, that no results of the irrevocable past two years are settled, that not even the title to our new possessions is settled, and never will be until it is settled according to their notions, you can answer that then the title to Massachusetts is not settled, nor the title to a square mile of land in most of the States from ocean to ocean. Over practically none of it did we assume sovereignty by the consent of the inhabitants.

Where is your Real Interest?

Quite possibly these controversies may embarrass the Government and threaten the security of the party in power. New and perplexing responsibilities often do that. But is it to the interest of the sincere and patriotic among the discontented to produce either result? The one thing sure is that no party in power in this country will dare abandon these new possessions. That being so, do those of you who regret it prefer to lose all influence over the outcome? While you are repining over what is beyond recall, events are moving on. If you do not help shape them, others, without your high principle and purity of motive, may. Can you wonder if, while you are harassing the Administration with impracticable demands for an abandonment of territory which the American people will not let go, less unselfish influences are busy presenting candidates for all the offices in its organization? If the friends of a proper civil service persist in chasing the ignis fatuus of persuading Americans to throw away territory, while the politicians are busy crowding their favorites into the territorial offices, who will feel free from self-reproach at the results? Grant that the situation is bad. Can there be a doubt of the duty to make the best of it? Do you ask how? By being an active patriot, not a passive one. By exerting, and exerting now when it is needed, every form of influence, personal, social, political, moral,—the influence of the clubs, the Chambers of Commerce, the manufactories, the colleges, and the churches,—in favor of the purest, the ablest, the most scientific, the most disinterested—in a word, the best possible civil service for the new possessions that the conscience and the capacity of America can produce, with the most liberal use of all the material available from native sources.

I have done. I have no wish to argue, to defend, or to attack. I have sought only to point out what I conceive to be the present danger and the present duty. It is not to be doubted that all such considerations will summon you to the high resolve that you will neither shame the Republic by shirking the task its own victory entails, nor despoil the Republic by abandoning its rightful possessions, nor degrade the Republic by admissions of unfit elements to its Union; but that you will honor it, enrich it, ennoble it, by doing your utmost to make the administration of these possessions worthy of the Nation that Washington founded and Lincoln preserved. My last word is an appeal to stand firm and stand all together for the Continental Union and for a pure civil service for the Islands.

X

OUR NEW INTERESTS

This address was delivered on Charter Day at the University of California, on March 23, 1900.

OUR NEW INTERESTS

My subject has been variously stated in your different newspapers as "Current National Questions," or "The Present National Question," or "General Expositions; Not on Anything in Particular." When your President honored me with his invitation to a duty so high and so sudden that it might almost be dignified by the name of a draft, he gave me nearly equal license. I was to speak "on anything growing out of the late war with Spain."

How that war resembles the grippe! You remember the medical definition by an authority no less high than our present distinguished Secretary of State. "The grippe," said Colonel Hay, "is that disease in which, after you have been cured, you get steadily worse every day of your convalescence"! There are people of so little faith as to say that this exactly describes the late war with Spain.

If one is to speak at all of its present aspects, on this high-day of your University year, he should do so only as a patriot, not as a partizan. But he cannot avoid treading on ground where the ashes are yet warm, and discussing questions which, in spite of the present intermingling of party lines and confusion of party ideas, will presently be found the very battle-ground of campaign oratory and hostile hosts. You will credit me, I hope, with sufficient respect for the proprieties of this platform to avoid partizan arguments, under the warrant of your distinguished President to discuss national questions from any point of view that a patriot can take. It is profoundly to be regretted that on these questions, which pure patriotism alone should weigh and decide, mere partizanship is already grasping the scales. One thing at least I may venture to promise before this audience of scholars and gentlemen on this Charter Day of your great University: I shall ask the Democrat of the present day to agree with me no farther than Thomas Jefferson went, and the Republican of the day no farther than Abraham Lincoln went. To adapt from a kindred situation a phrase by the greatest popular orator of my native State, and, I still like to think, one of the greatest of the country in this century,—a phrase applied by him to the compromise measures of 1848, but equally fitting to-day,—"If we are forced to part company with some here whom it has been our pleasure and pride to follow in the past, let us console ourselves by the reflection that we are following in the footsteps of the fathers and saviors of the Republic, their garments dyed with the blood of the Red Sea, through which they led us out of the land of bondage, their locks still moist with the mists of the Jordan, across which they brought us to this land of liberty."[16]

To be Taken for Granted now.

Yet, even with those from whom we must thus part company there are elemental truths of the situation on which we must still agree. Some things reasonable men may take for granted—some that surely have been settled in the conflict of arms, of diplomacy, and of debate since the spring of 1898. Regret them if you choose, but do not, like children, seek to make them as though they were not, by shutting your eyes to them.

The new territories in the West Indies and the East are ours, to have and to hold, by the supreme law of the land, and by a title which the whole civilized world recognizes and respects. We shall not speedily get rid of them—whoever may desire it. The American people are in no mood to give them back to Spain, or to sell them, or to abandon them. We have all the power we need to acquire and to govern them. Whatever theories men may quote from Mr. Calhoun or from Mr. Chief Justice Taney, the uniform conduct of the National Administration throughout a century, under whatever party, justifies the triumphant declaration of Daniel Webster to Mr. Calhoun, over half a century ago, and the consenting opinions of the courts for a long term since, down to the very latest in the line, by your own Judge Morrow, to the effect, in a word, that this Government, like every other one in the world, has power to acquire "territory and other property" anywhere, and govern it as it pleases.[17]

On these points I make bold to repeat what I felt warranted in saying a fortnight ago within sight of Bunker Hill—that there is every evidence that the American people have distinctly and definitely made up their minds. They have not been persuaded and they cannot be persuaded that this is an inferior government, incapable of any duty Providence may send its way—duties which other nations could discharge, but we cannot. So I venture to affirm the impossibility that any party in power, whether the present one or its opponent, could soon, if ever, abandon one foot of the territory gained in the late war.

We are gathered on another old Spanish territory taken by our country in war. It shows what Americans do with such acquisitions. Before you expect to see Porto Rico given back to Spain or the Philippines abandoned to Aguinaldo, wait till we are ready to declare, as Daniel Webster did in the Senate, that this California of your pride and glory is "not worth a dollar," and throw back the worthless thing on the hands of unoffending Mexico. Till then, let us as practical and sensible men recognize that what is past is settled.

Duty First; but then Interest also.

Thus far have we come in these strange courses and to these unexpected and unwelcome tasks by following, at each succeeding emergency, the path of clear, absolute, and unavoidable duty. The only point in the whole national line of conduct, from the spring of 1898 on to this March morning of 1900, at which our Government could have stopped with honor, was at the outset. I, for one, would gladly have stopped there. How was it then with some at the West who are discontented now? Shake not your gory locks at me or at my fellow-citizens in the East. You cannot say we did it. In 1898, just as a few years earlier in the debate about Venezuela, the loudest calls for a belligerent policy came not from the East, "the cowardly, commercial East," as we were sometimes described, but from the patriotic and warlike West. The farther West you came, the louder the cry for war, till it reached its very climax on what we used to call the frontier, and was sent thundering Eastward upon the National Capital in rolling reverberations from the Sierras and the Rockies which few public men cared to defy. At that moment, perhaps, if this popular and congressional demand had not pushed us forward, we might have stopped with honor—certainly not later. From the day war was flagrant down to this hour there has been no forward step which a peremptory national or international obligation did not require. To the mandate alone of Duty, stern daughter of the voice of God, the American people have bowed, as, let us hope, they always will. It is not true that, in the final decision as to any one step in the great movement hitherto, our interests have been first or chiefly considered.

But in all these constitutional discussions to which we have referred, one clause in the Constitution has been curiously thrust aside. The framers placed it on the very forefront of the edifice they were rearing, and there declared for our instruction and guidance that "the people do ordain and establish this Constitution ... to promote the general welfare." By what right do statesmen now venture to think that they can leave our national interests out of the account? Who and where is the sentimentalist who arraigns us for descending to too sordid a level when we recognize our interest to hold what the discharge of duty has placed in our hand? Since when has it been statesmanship to shut our eyes to the interests of our own country, and patriotism to consider only the interests or the wishes of others? For my own part, I confess to a belief in standing up first for my own, and find it difficult to cherish much respect for the man who won't: first for my own family rather than some other man's; first for my own city and State rather than for somebody else's; first for my own country—first, please God! for the United States of America. And so, having in the past, too fully, perhaps, and more than once, considered the question of our new possessions in the light of our duty, I propose now to look at them further, and unblushingly, in the light of our interests.

The Old Faith of Californians.

Which way do your interests lie? Which way do the interests of California and the city of San Francisco lie?

Three or four days ago, when your President honored me with the summons I am now obeying, there came back to me a vague memory of the visions cherished by the men you rate the highest in California, your "Pioneers" and "Forty-Niners," as to the future of the empire they were founding on this coast. There lingered in my mind the flavor at least of an old response by a California public man to the compliment a "tenderfoot" New-Yorker, in the innocence of his heart, had intended to pay, when he said that with this splendid State, this glorious harbor, and the Pacific Ocean, you have all the elements to build up here the New York of the West. The substance of the Californian's reply was that, through mere lack of knowledge of the country to which he belonged, the well-meaning New-Yorker had greatly underrated the future that awaited San Francisco—that long before Macaulay's New-Zealander had transferred himself from the broken arches of London Bridge to those of Brooklyn, it would be the pride and boast of the denizens of those parts that New York had held its own so finely as still to be fairly called the San Francisco of the East!

While the human memory is the most tenacious and nearest immortal of all things known to us, it is also at times the most elusive. Even with the suggestions of Mr. Hittell and the friendly files of the Mechanics' Library, I did not succeed in finding that splendid example of San Francisco faith which my memory had treasured. Yet I found some things not very unlike it to show what manner of men they were that laid the foundations of this commonwealth on the Pacific, what high hopes sustained them, and what radiant future they confidently anticipated.

Here, for example, was Mr. William A. Howard, whom I found declaring, not quite a third of a century ago, that San Francisco would yet be the largest American city on the largest ocean in the world. At least, so he is reported in "The Bulletin" and "The Call," though "The Alta" puts it with an "if," its report reading: "If the development of commerce require that the largest ocean shall have the largest city, then it would follow that as the Atlantic is smaller than the Pacific, so in the course of years New York will be smaller than San Francisco."

And here, again, was Mr. Delos Lake, maintaining that the "United States is now on a level with the most favored nations; that its geographical position, its line of palatial steamers established on the Pacific Ocean by American enterprise, and soon to be followed by ocean telegraphs, must before long render this continent the proper avenue of commerce between Europe and Asia, and raise this metropolis of the Pacific to the loftiest height of monetary power."

There was a reason, too, widely held by the great men of the day, whose names have passed into history, for some such faith. Thus an old Californian of high and happy fame, Major-General Henry W.

Halleck, speaking of San Francisco, said: "Standing here on the extreme Western verge of the Republic, overlooking the coast of Asia and occupying the future center of trade and commerce of the two worlds,... if that civilization which so long has moved westward with the Star of Empire is now, purified by the principles of true Christianity, to go on around the world until it reaches the place of its origin and makes the Orient blossom again with its benign influences, San Francisco must be made the abutment, and International Law the bridge, by which it will cross the Pacific Ocean. The enterprise of the merchants of California has already laid the foundation of the abutments; diplomacy and steam and telegraph companies are rapidly accumulating material for the construction of the bridge." Thus far Halleck. But have the Californians of this generation abandoned the bridge? Are we to believe those men of to-day who tell us it is not worth crossing?

Here, again, was Eugene Casserly, speaking of right for the California Democracy of that date. Writing with deliberation more than a quarter of a century ago, he said: "We expect to stand on equal grounds with the most favored of nations. We ask no more in the contest for that Eastern trade which has always heretofore been thought to carry with it the commercial supremacy of the globe. America asks only a fair field, even as against her oldest and most formidable rivals. Nature, and our position as the nearest neighbors to eastern Asia, separated from her only by the great highways of the ocean, have placed in our hands all the advantages that we need.... Favored by vicinity, by soil and climate on our own territory, with a people inferior to none in enterprise and vigor, without any serious rivals anywhere, all this Pacific coast is ours or is our tributary.... We hold as ours the great ocean that so lately rolled in solitary grandeur from the equator to the pole. In the changes certain to be effected in the currents of finance, of exchange, and of trade, by the telegraph and the railroads, bringing the financial centers of Europe and of the United States by way of San Francisco within a few weeks of the ports of China and of the East, San Francisco must become at no distant day the banker, the factor, and the carrier of the trade of eastern Asia and the Pacific, to an extent to which it is difficult to assign limits." Are the people now lacking in the enterprise and vigor which Mr. Casserly claimed for them?

Have the limits he scorned been since assigned, and do the Californians of to-day assent to the restriction?

Take yet another name, treasured, I know, on the roll of California's most worthy servants, another Democrat. Governor Haight, only a third of a century ago, said: "I see in the near future a vast commerce springing up between the Chinese Empire and the nations of the West; an interchange of products and manufactures mutually beneficial; the watchword of progress and the precepts of a pure religion uttered to the ears of a third of the human race." And addressing some representatives of that vast region, he added, with a burst of fine confidence in the supremacy of San Francisco's position: "As Chief Magistrate of this Western State of the Nation, I welcome you to the territory of the Republic,... in no selfish or narrow spirit, either of personal advantage or seeking exclusive privileges for our own over the other nations; and so, in the name of commerce, of civilization, of progress, of humanity, and of religion, on behalf not merely of California or America, but of Europe and of mankind, I bid you and your associates welcome and God-speed."

Perhaps this may be thought merely an exuberant hospitality. Let me quote, then, from the same man, speaking again as the Governor of the State, at the Capitol of the State, in the most careful oration of his life: "What shall be said of the future of California? Lift your eyes and expand your conceptions to take in the magnitude of her destiny. An empire in area, presenting advantages and attractions to the people of the Eastern States and Europe far beyond those presented by any other State or Territory—who shall set limits to her progress, or paint in fitting colors the splendor of her future?... Mismanagement may at times retard her progress, but if the people of California are true to themselves, this State is destined to a high position, not only among her sister States, but among the commonwealths of the world,... when her ships visit every shore, and her merchant princes control the commerce of the great ocean and the populous countries upon its borders."

Was Governor Haight alone, or was he in advance of his time? Go yet farther back, to the day when Judge Nathaniel Bennett was assigned by the people of San Francisco to the task of delivering the oration when they celebrated the admission of California into the

Union, on October 29, 1850: "Judging from the past, what have we not a right to expect in the future? The world has never witnessed anything equal or similar to our career hitherto.... Our State is a marvel to ourselves, and a miracle to the rest of the world. Nor is the influence of California confined within her own borders.... The islands nestled in the embrace of the Pacific have felt the quickening breath of her enterprise.... She has caused the hum of busy life to be heard in the wilderness where rolls the Oregon, and where until recently was heard no sound save his own dashings. Even the wall of Chinese exclusiveness has been broken down, and the children of the Sun have come forth to view the splendors of her achievements.... It is all but a foretaste of the future.... The world's trade is destined soon to be changed.... The commerce of Asia and the islands of the Pacific, instead of pursuing the ocean track by the way of Cape Horn or the Cape of Good Hope, or even taking the shorter route of the Isthmus of Darien or the Isthmus of Tehuantepec, will enter the Golden Gate of California and deposit its riches in the lap of our city.... New York will then become what London now is—the great central point of exchange, the heart of trade, the force of whose contraction and expansion will be felt throughout every artery of the commercial world; and San Francisco will then stand the second city of America.... The responsibility rests upon us whether this first American State of the Pacific shall in youth and ripe manhood realize the promise of infancy. We may cramp her energies and distort her form, or we may make her a rival even of the Empire State of the Atlantic. The best wishes of Americans are with us. They expect that the Herculean youth will grow to a Titan in his manhood."

Nor was even Judge Bennett the pioneer of such ideas. Long before he spoke, or before the Stars and Stripes had been raised over Yerbabuena, as far back as in 1835, the English people and the British Government had been advised by Alexander Forbes that "The situation of California for intercourse with other countries and its capacity for commerce—should it ever be possessed by a numerous and industrious population—are most favorable. The port of San Francisco for size and safety is hardly surpassed by any in the world; it is so situated as to be made the center of the commercial relations which may take place between Asia and the western coast of America.... The vessels of the Spanish Philippines Company on their passage from Manila to San Blas and Acapulco generally called at Monterey for refreshments and orders.... Thus it appears as if California was designed by nature to be the medium of connecting commercially Asia with America, and as the depot of the trade between these two vast continents, which possess the elements of unbounded commercial interchange; the one overflowing with all the rich and luxurious commodities always characteristic of the East, the other possessing a superabundance of the precious metals and other valuable products to give in exchange.... If ever a route across the Isthmus shall be opened, California will then be one of the most interesting commercial situations in the world; it would in that case be the rendezvous for all vessels engaged in the trade between Europe and Asia by that route. It is nearly mid-voyage between these two countries, and would furnish provisions and all naval supplies in the most ample abundance, and most probably would become a mart for the interchange of the commodities of the three continents."

Has the State Lost Heart and Shriveled?

Let no man fancy that these sometimes exuberant expressions of a noble and far-seeing faith by your own predecessors and by a prescient foreigner have been revived in derision or even in doubt. Those were the days when, if some were for a party, at any rate all were for the State. These were great men, far-seeing, courageous, patriotic, the men of Forty-nine, who in such lofty spirit and with such high hope laid the foundation of this empire on the Pacific. Distance did not disturb them, nor difficulties discourage. There sits on your platform to-day a man who started from New York to California by what he thought the quickest route in December, 1848; went south from the Isthmus as the only means of catching a ship for the north, and finally entered this harbor, by the way of Chile, in June, 1849. He could go now to Manila thrice over and back in less time. And yet there are Californians of this day who profess to shrink in alarm from the remoteness and inaccessibility of our new possessions! Has the race shriveled under these summer skies? Has it grown old before its time; is its natural strength abated? Are the old energy and the old courage gone? Has the soul of this people shrunk within them? Or is it only that there are strident voices from

California, sounding across the Sierras and the Rockies, that misrepresent and shame a State whose sons are not unworthy of their fathers?

The arm of the Californian has not been shortened, that he cannot reach out. The salt has not left him, that he cannot occupy and possess the great ocean that the Lord has given him. Nor has he forgotten the lesson taught by the history of his own race (and of the greatest nations of the world), that oceans no longer separate—they unite. There are no protracted and painful struggles to build a Pacific railroad for your next great step. The right of way is assured, the grading is done, the rails are laid. You have but to buy your rolling-stock at the Union Iron Works, draw up your time-table, and begin business. Or do you think it better that your Pacific railroad should end in the air? Is a six-thousand-mile extension to a through line worthless? Can your Scott shipyards only turn out men-of-war? Can your Senator Perkins only run ships that creep along the coast? Is the broad ocean too deep for him or too wide?

New Fields and the Need for them.

Contiguous land gives a nation cohesion; but it is the water that brings other nations near. The continent divides you from customers beyond the mountains; but the ocean unites you with the whole boundless, mysterious Orient. There you find a population of over six hundred millions of souls, between one fourth and one third of the inhabitants of the globe. You are not at a disadvantage in trading with them because they have the start of you in manufactures or skill or capital, as you would be in the countries to which the Atlantic leads. They offer you the best of all commerce—that with people less advanced, exchanging the products of different zones, a people awakening to the complex wants of a civilization that is just stirring them to a new life.

Have you considered what urgent need there will be for those new fields? It is no paltry question of an outlet for the surplus products of a mere nation of seventy-five millions that confronts you. Your mathematical professors will tell you that, at the ratio of increase established in this Nation by the census returns for the century just closing, its population would amount during the next century to the bewildering and incomprehensible figure of twelve hundred millions. The ratio, of course, will not be maintained, since the exceptional circumstances that caused it cannot continue. But no one gives reasons why it should not be half as great. Suppose it to turn out only one fourth as great. Is it the part of statesmanship—is it even the part of every-day, matter-of-fact common sense—to reject or despise these Oriental openings for the products of this people of three hundred million souls the Twentieth Century would need to nourish within our borders? Our total annual trade with China now—with this customer whom the friendly ocean is ready to bring to your very doors—is barely twenty millions. That would be a commerce of the gross amount of six and two third cents for each inhabitant of our country in the next century, with that whole vast region adjoining you, wherein dwell one fourth of the human race!

Even the Spanish trade with the Philippines was thirty millions. They are merely our stepping-stone. But would a wise man kick the stepping-stone away?

The New Blood Felt.

San Francisco is exceptionally prosperous now. So is the State of California. Why? Partly, no doubt, because you are sharing the prosperity which blesses the whole country. But is that all? What is this increase in the shipping at your wharves? What was the meaning of those crowded columns of business statistics your newspapers proudly printed last New Year's?—what the significance of the increase in exports and imports, far beyond mere army requirements? Why is every room taken in your big buildings? What has crowded your docks, filled your streets, quickened your markets, rented your stores and dwellings, sent all this new blood pulsing through your veins—made you like the worn Richelieu when, in that moment, there entered his spent veins the might of France?

Was it the rage you have witnessed among some of your own leaders against everything that has been done during the past two years—the warning against everything that is about to be done? Was it the proof of our unworthiness and misdeeds, to which we all penitentially listened, as so eloquently set forth from the high places of light and leading—the long lamentation over how on almost every field we had shown our incapacity; how unfit we were to govern cities, unfit to govern territories, unfit to govern Indians, unfit to govern ourselves—how, in good old theological phrase, we were from head to foot a mass of national wounds and bruises and putrefying sores, and there was no health in us? Was it the demonstration that what we needed was to sit under the live-oaks and "develop the individual man," nor dare to look beyond? Was it the forgetfulness that muscles grow strong only with exercise; that it is the duties of manhood that take the acrid humors out of a youth's blood; that it is great responsibility, manfully met, not cowardly evaded, that sobers and steadies and ennobles?

Some one has lately been quoting Lincoln's phrase, "We cannot escape history." It is a noble and inspiring thought. Most of us dare not look for a separate appearance at that greatest of human bars—may hope only to be reckoned in bulk with the multitude. But even so, however it may be with others on this coast, I, for one, want to be counted with those who had faith in my countrymen; who did not think them incapable of tasks which duty imposed and to which other nations had been equal; who did not disparage their powers or distrust their honest intentions or urge them to refuse their opportunities; to be counted with those who at least had open eyes when they stood in the Golden Gate!

Wards or Full Partners.

I do not doubt—you do not doubt—they are the majority. They will prevail. What Duty requires us to take, an enlightened regard for our own interests will require us to hold. The islands will not be thrown away. The American people have made up their minds on that point, if on nothing else.

Well, then, how shall the islands be treated? Are they to be our wards, objects of our duty and our care; or are they to be our full partners? We may as well look that question straight in the face. There is no way around it, or over or under or out of it; and no way of aimlessly and helplessly shuffling it off on the future, for it presses in the legislation of Congress to-day. Wards, flung on our hands by the shipwreck of Spain, helpless, needy, to be cared for and brought up and taught to stand alone as far as they can; or full partners with us in the government and administration of the priceless heritage of our fathers, the peerless Republic of the world and of all the centuries—that is the question!

Men often say—I have even heard it within a week on this coast—that all this is purely imaginary; that nobody favors their admission as States. Let us see. An ounce of fact in a matter of such moment is worth tons of random denial. Within the month a distinguished and experienced United States Senator from the North has announced that he sees no reason why Porto Rico should not be a State. Within the same period one of the leading religious journals of the continent has declared that it would be a selfish and brutal tyranny that would exclude Porto Rico from Statehood. Only a few weeks earlier one of our ablest generals, now commanding a department in one of our dependencies, a laureled hero of two wars, has officially reported to the Government in favor of steps for the admission of Cuba as a State. On every hand rise cries that in any event they cannot and must not be dependencies. Some of these are apparently for mere partizan effect, but others are the obvious promptings of a sincere and high-minded, however mistaken, conviction.

I shall venture, then, to consider it as a real and not an abstract question,—"academic," I think it is the fad of these later days to say,—and I propose again (and again unblushingly) to consider it from what has been called a low and sordid point of view—so low, in fact, so unworthy the respect of latter-day altruistic philosophers, that it merely concerns the interests of our country!

For I take it that if there is one subject on which this Union has a right to consult its own interests and inclinations, it is on the question of admitting new States, or of putting territory in a position where it can ever claim or expect admission; just as the one subject on which nobody disputes the right of a mercantile firm to follow its own inclinations is on that of taking in some unfortunate business man as a partner; or the right of an individual to follow his own inclinations about marrying some needy spinster he may have felt it a duty to befriend. Because they are helpless and needy and on our hands, must we take them into partnership? Because we are going to help them, are we bound to marry them?

The Porto Rican Question.

Partly through mere inadvertence, but partly also through crafty design, the wave of generous sympathy for the suffering little island of Porto Rico which has been sweeping over the country has come very near being perverted into the means of turning awry the policy and permanent course of a great Nation. To relieve the temporary distress by recognizing the Porto Ricans as citizens, and by an extension of the Dingley tariff to Porto Rico as a matter of constitutional right, foreclosed the whole question.

I know it is said, plausibly enough, in some quarters, that Congress cannot foreclose the question,—has nothing to do with it, in fact,—but that it is a matter to be settled only by the Supreme Law of the land, of which Congress is merely the servant. The point need not be disputed. But it is an unquestioned part of the Supreme Law of the land, as authoritative within its sphere and as binding as any clause in the Constitution itself, which declares, in the duly ratified Treaty of Paris, that the whole question of the civil rights and political status of the inhabitants in this newly acquired property of ours shall be reserved for the decision of Congress! Let those who invoke the Supreme Law of the land learn and bow to it.

As to the mere duty of prompt and ample relief for the distress in Porto Rico, there is happily not a shade of difference of opinion among the seventy-five millions of our inhabitants. Nor was the free-trade remedy, so vehemently recommended, important enough in itself to provoke serious objection or delay. Cynical observers might find, indeed, a gentle amusement in noting how in the name of humanity the blessings of free trade were invoked by means of the demand for an immediate application of the highest protective tariff known to the history of economics! The very men who denounce this tariff as a Chinese wall are the men who demand its application. They say, "Give Porto Rico free trade," but what their proposal means is, "Deprive Porto Rico of free trade, and put her within the barbarous Chinese wall." Their words sound like offering her the liberty of trade with all the world, but mean forbidding her to trade with anybody except the United States.

Importance of the Question.

The importance of the question from an economic point of view has been ludicrously exaggerated on both sides. The original proposal would have in itself done far less harm than its opponents imagined and far less good than its supporters hoped. Yet to the extent of its influence it would have been a step backward. It would have been the rejection of the modern and scientific colonial method, and the adoption instead of the method which has resulted in the most backward, the least productive, and the least prosperous colonies in the world—the method, in a word, of Spain herself. For the Spanish tariff, in fact, made with some little reference to colonial interests, we should merely have substituted our own tariff, made with sole reference to our own interests. A more distinct piece of blacksmith work in economic legislation for a helpless, lonely little island in the mid-Atlantic could not well be imagined. What had poor Porto Rico done, that she should be fenced in from all the Old World by an elaborate and highly complicated system of duties upon imports, calculated to protect the myriad varying manufactures and maintain the high wages of this vast new continent, and as little adapted to Porto Rico's simple needs as is a Jorgensen repeater for the uses of a kitchen clock? Why at the same stroke must she be crushed, as she would have been if the Constitution were extended to her, by a system of internal taxation, which we ourselves prefer to regard as highly exceptional, on tobacco, on tobacco-dealers, on bank-checks, on telegraph and telephone messages, on bills of lading, bills of exchange, leases, mortgages, life-insurance, passenger tickets, medicines, legacies, inheritances, mixed flour, and so on and so on, ad infinitum, ad nauseam? Did she deserve so badly of us that, even in a hurry, we should do this thing to her in the name of humanity?

All the English-speaking world, outside some members of the United States Congress perhaps, long since found a more excellent way. It is simplicity itself. It legislates for a community like Porto Rico with reference to the situation and wants of that community—not with reference to somebody else. It applies to Porto Rico a system devised for Porto Rico—not one devised for a distant and vastly larger country, with totally different situation and wants. It makes no effort to exploit Porto Rico for the benefit of another country. It does make a studied and scientific effort from the Porto Rico point of view (not from that of temporary Spanish holders of the present stocks of Porto Rican products) to see what system will impose the lightest burdens and bring the greatest benefits on Porto

Rico herself. The result of that conscientious inquiry may be the discovery that the very best thing to provide for the wants and promote the prosperity of that little community out in the Atlantic Ocean is to bestow upon them the unmixed boon of the high protective Dingley tariff devised for the United States of America. If so, give them the Dingley tariff, and give it straight. If, on the other hand, it should be found that a lower and simpler revenue system, better adapted to a community which has practically no manufactures to protect, with freedom to trade on equal terms with all the world, would impose upon them lighter burdens and bring them greater benefits, then give them that. If it should be further found that, following this, such a system of reciprocal rebates as both Cuba and the United States thought mutually advantageous in the late years of Spanish rule, would be useful to Porto Rico, then give them that. But, in any case, the starting-point should be the needs of Porto Rico herself, intelligently studied and conscientiously met—not the blacksmith's offhand attempt to fit on her head, like a rusty iron pot, an old system made for other needs, other industries, a distant land, and another people.

And beyond and above all, give her the best system for her situation and wants, whether it be our Dingley tariff or some other, because it is the best for her and is therefore our duty—not because it is ours, and therefore, under the Constitution of the United States, her right and her fate. The admission of that ill-omened and unfounded claim would be, at the bar of politics, a colossal blunder; at the bar of patriotism, a colossal crime.

Political Aspect of the Constitutional Claim.

The politics of it need not greatly concern this audience or long detain you.

But the facts are interesting. If Porto Rico, instead of belonging to us, is a part of us, so are the Philippines. Our title to each is exactly the same. So are Guam and the Sandwich Islands, if not also Samoa; and so will be Cuba if she comes, or any other West India Island.

First, then, you are proposing to open the ports of the United States directly to the tropical products of the two greatest archipelagos of the world, and indirectly, through the Open Door we have pledged in the Philippines, to all the products of all the world! You guarantee directly to the cheap labor of these tropical regions, and indirectly, but none the less bindingly, to the cheap labor of the world, free admission of their products to this continent, in unrestricted competition with our own higher-paid labor. And as your whole tariff system is thus plucked up by the roots, you must resort to direct taxation for the expenses of the General Government.

Secondly, as if this were not enough, you have made these tropical laborers citizens,—Chinese, half-breeds, pagans, and all,—and have given them the unquestionable and inalienable right to follow their products across the ocean if they like, flood our labor market, and compete in person on our own soil with our own workmen.

Is that the feast to be set before the laboring men of this country? Is that the real inwardness of the Trojan horse pushed forward against our tariff wall, in the name of humanity, to suffering Porto Rico? What a programme for the wise humanitarians who have been bewitching the world with noble statesmanship at Washington to propose laying before the organized labor of this country as their chosen platform for the approaching Presidential campaign! They need have no fear the intelligent workingmen of America will fail to appreciate the sweet boon they offer.

The Patriotic Aspect of it.

But if the question thus raised at the bar of politics may seem to some only food for laughter, that at the bar of patriotism is matter for tears. If the islanders are already citizens, then they are entitled to the future of citizens. If the territory is already an integral part of the United States, then by all our practice and traditions it has the right to admission in States of suitable size and population. Is it said we could keep them out as we have kept out sparsely settled New Mexico? How long do you expect to keep New Mexico out, or Oklahoma, or Arizona? What luck did you have in keeping out others—even Utah, with its bar sinister of the twin relic of barbarism? How long would it take your politicians of the baser sort to combine for the admission of the islands whose electoral votes they had reason to think they could control?

But it is said that Porto Rico deserves admission anyway, because we are bound by the volunteered assurance of General Miles that they should have the rights of American citizens. Perhaps; though there is no evidence that he meant more, or that they thought he meant more, than such rights as American citizens everywhere enjoy, even in the District of Columbia—equal laws, security of life and property, freedom from arbitrary arrests, local self-government, in a word, the civil rights which the genius of our Government secures to all under our control who are capable of exercising them. If he did mean more, or if they thought he meant more, did that entitle him to anticipate his chief and override in casual military proclamation the Supreme Law of the land whose commission he bore? Or did it entitle them to suppose that he could?

But Porto Rico received the irresistible army of General Miles so handsomely, and is so unfortunate and so little! Reasons all for consideration, certainly, for care, for generosity—but not for starting the avalanche, on the theory that after it has got under only a little headway we can still stop it if we want to. Who thinks he can lay his hand on the rugged edge of the Muir Glacier and compel it to advance no farther? Who believes that we can admit this little island from the mid-Atlantic, a third of the way over to Africa, and then reject nearer and more valuable islands when they come? The famous law of political gravitation which John Quincy Adams prophetically announced three quarters of a century ago will then be acting with ever-increasing force. And, at any rate, beside Porto Rico, and with the same title, stand the Philippines!

Regard, I beg of you, in the calm white light that befits these cloistered retreats of sober thought, the degradation of the Republic thus coolly anticipated by the men that assure us we have no possessions whose people are not entitled under our Constitution to citizenship and ultimately to Statehood! Surely to an audience of scholars and patriots like this not one word need be added. Emboldened by the approval you have so generously expressed, I venture to close by assuming without hesitation that you will not dishonor your Government by evading its duty, nor betray it by forcing unfit partners upon it, nor rob it by blind and perverse neglect of its interests.

May I not go further, and vouch for you, as Californians, that the faith of the fathers has not forsaken the sons—that you still believe in the possibilities of the good land the Lord has given you, and mean to work them out; that you know what hour the national clock has struck, and are not mistaking this for the Eighteenth Century; that you will bid the men who have made that mistake, the men of little faith, the shirkers, the doubters, the carpers, the grumblers, begone, like Diogenes, to their tubs—aye, better his instruction and require these his followers to get out of your light? For, lo! yet another century is upon you, before which even the marvels of the Nineteenth are to grow pale. As of old, light breaks from the east, but now also, for you, from the farther East. It circles the world in both directions, like the flag it is newly gilding now with its tropic beams. The dawn of the Twentieth Century bursts upon you without needing to cross the Sierras, and bathes at once in its golden splendors, with simultaneous effulgence, the Narrows of Sandy Hook and the peerless portals of the Golden Gate.

XI

"UNOFFICIAL INSTRUCTIONS"

This speech was delivered at the Farewell Banquet given by over four hundred citizens of San Francisco to the second Philippine Commission, on the eve of their sailing for Manila, at the Palace Hotel, April 12, 1900. The title is adopted from the phrase used by the President of the Commission in his response; to which a leading journal of the Pacific coast, "The Seattle Post-Intelligencer," promptly added that the address "spoke for the whole people of the United States," and was "the concrete expression of a desire that animates nine tenths of all our citizens." Judge Taft frankly stated his concurrence in the views expressed (though he held some legal doubts as to whether the Constitution of the United States did not extend, ex proprio vigore, to the new possessions), and he pledged the Commission against the influence of political considerations.

"UNOFFICIAL INSTRUCTIONS"

The kindness of your call shall not be misinterpreted or taken advantage of. Quite enough of my voice has been heard in the land, and that very recently, as some of you can testify to your cost. There are others here with far greater claims upon your attention, and I promise to be as brief as heretofore I have been prolix.

The occasion is understood to be primarily one of congratulation and personal good will. It is evident that San Francisco thinks well of the Pacific coast member of this Commission, and none the worse because he seems to have been chosen for the post merely on account of his being peculiarly fit for it. The city gladly takes the rest of you on faith, believing that the same rule of selection must have been applied in the cases with which it has not the happiness to be quite so familiar.

But it is an occasion, I am authoritatively assured, of no political significance whatever. It embraces in its comprehensive impulse of greeting and good wishes Republicans and Democrats and Dewey men; men who hold the offices, men who want the offices, and men who say, "A plague on both your houses!"—men who indorse the course of the Administration, and men who believe the acquisition of the Philippines a mistake. I shall not attempt to disguise from you the fact that this last is not an opinion that I individually hold. Still, I can respect the convictions of those who do.

But evidently we can have no concurrence to-night on our extra-continental policy, since the differences are so wide on vital points. Yet the organizers of this testimonial made no mistake. There is a common ground for our meeting. We are all citizens of the Republic, grateful for our high privilege and solicitous that the Republic shall take no harm—all Americans, proud of the name and eager that it shall never be stained by base or unworthy acts. There is no one here, of whatever political faith or lack of faith, who is not a patriot, anxious for our country on these new and untried paths it must walk—most desirous that all its ways may prove ways of pleasantness and all its paths lead to honorable peace.

Well, then, gentlemen, what is it that a company thus divided in opinion, and united only in patriotic aspirations, can agree in looking to this Commission for? What do the American people in general, and without distinction of party, look to them for?

Did I hear a public opponent but personal friend over there murmur as his reply, "Not much of anything"? Alas! we may as well recognize that there are political augurs who are ready to give just that as their horoscope, and even point to their useful predecessor, the last Commission, for presumptive proof! In fact, there are occasional grumblers who would look for more from them if they were fewer. These skeptical critics recognize that sometimes in a multitude of counselors there may be safety, but also recall the maxim that councils of war never fight. If the truth must be whispered in the ear of the Commissioners, there are here and there very sincere, capable people who are growing a bit weary of a multiplicity of commissions. They say—so cynical are they—that, in all ages and countries, the easiest method of evading or postponing a difficult problem has been to appoint a commission on it and thus prolong the circumlocution.

For a first thing, then, on which we are all united, we look hopefully to our guests to redeem the character of this mode of government by commission. For we assume that they are sent out to the archipelago to govern; and just at present we don't know of any part of the country's possessions that seems more in need of government.

We all unite in regarding them as setting sail, not only charged with the national interests, but dignified and ennobled by a guardianship of the national honor. Thus we are trying to put ourselves in Emerson's state of mind about a certain notable young poet, and unite in hoping that, to use his well-known phrase, we greet them at the beginning of a great career.

We certainly unite in earnestly wishing that they may make the best of a situation which none of us wholly like, and many dislike with all their hearts: the best of it for the country which, by good management or bad, rightfully or wrongfully, is at any rate clearly and in the eyes of the whole world now responsible for the outcome; and the best of it, no less, for the distracted people thrown upon our hands.

We cannot well help uniting in the further hope that their first success will be the re-establishment of order throughout regions lately filled with violence and bloodshed; and that they can then bring about a system of just and swift punishment for future crimes of disorder, since all experience in those regions and among those people shows that the neglect to enforce such punishment is itself the gravest and cruelest of crimes.

Nor can any one here help uniting in the hope that their next and crowning success will some way be attained in the preservation and extension of those great civil rights whose growth is the distinction, the world over, of Anglo-Saxon civilization; whose consummate flower and fruitage are the glory of our own Government.

I am even bold enough to believe that, however it might have been twelve months ago, or but six months ago, there is no one here to-night, recognizing the changed circumstances now, who would think they could best secure those rights to all the people by calling back the leader who is in hiding, and his forces, which are scattered and disorganized, and by now abandoning to such revengeful rule the great majority of the islanders who have remained peaceful and orderly during our occupation. For the present, at least, we unite in recognizing that they are forced to retain that care themselves; forced to act in the common interest of all the people there, not in the sole interest of a warring faction in a single tribe—in the interest of all the islands for which we have accepted responsibility, not simply of the one, or of a part of the population on the one, that has made the most trouble.

There can be little disagreement in this company on the further proposition that, in like manner, they must act in the interest of all the people here. In the interest of the islanders, they will soon seek to raise the needed revenue in the way least burdensome and most beneficial to the islands; but in the interest of their country, we cannot expect them to begin by assuming that the only way to help the islanders is to throw products of tropic cheap labor into unrestricted competition with similar products of our highly paid labor. In the interest of the islanders, they will secure and guarantee the civil rights which belong to the very genius of American institutions; but in the interest of their country, they will not make haste to extend the privilege of American citizenship, and so, on the one hand, enable those peoples of the China Sea, Chinese or half-breed or what not, to flood our labor market in advance of any readiness at home to change our present laws of exclusion, while, on the other hand, opening the door to them as States in the Union to take part in the government of this continent. If, in the Providence of God, and in contempt of past judicial rulings, the Supreme Court should finally command it, this Commission, like every other branch of the Government, will obey. Till then we may be sure it will not, in sheer eagerness and joyfulness of heart, anticipate, or, as Wall Street speculators say, "discount," such a decree for national degradation. But in their own land, and, as far as may be, in accordance with their old customs and laws, the Commission will secure to them, if it is to win the success we all wish it, first every civil right we enjoy, and next the fullest measure of political rights and local self-government they are found capable of sustaining, with ordered liberty for all the people.

There, then, is the doom we have reason to expect this Commission to inflict on these temporarily turbulent wards of the Nation! First order; then justice; then American civil rights, not for a class, or a tribe, or a race, but for all the people; then local self-government.

But if your guests begin this task with the notion that they are the first officials of a free people ever given such work, and must therefore, American fashion, discover from the foundation for themselves,—if they fancy nobody ever dealt with semi-civilized Orientals till we stumbled on them in the Philippines,—they will waste precious time in costly experiments, if not fail outright. It isn't worth while thus to invent over again everything down to the very alphabet of work among such people. We can afford to abate the self-sufficiency of the almighty Yankee Nation enough to profit a little by the lessons other people have learned in going over the road before us.

From such lessons they will be sure to gather at once that if they now show a trace of timidity or hesitation in their firm and just course, because somebody has said something in Washington or on the stump, or because there is an election coming on, they will fail.

In fact, if they do not know now, as well as they know what soil they still stand on and what countrymen are about them, and if they do not act as if they knew, that, no matter what the politicians or the platforms say, and no matter what party comes into power, the American people have at present no notion of throwing these islands away, or abandoning them, or neglecting the care of them, they have not mastered the plainest part of their problem, and must fail.

Above all, if there is a trace of politics in their work, or of seeking for political effect at home, they will fail, and deserve to fail. In this most delicate and difficult task before them there is no salvation but in the scrupulous choice of the very best fitted agency available, in each particular case, for the particular work in hand. If they appoint one man, or encourage or silently submit to the appointment of one man, to responsible place in their service among these islanders, merely because he has been useful in politics at home, they will be organizing failure and discredit in advance.

But they will do no such things. Not so has this body of men been selected. Not such is the high appreciation of the opportunity offered that has led you, Mr. President of the Commission, to abandon your well-earned and distinguished place at home to begin a new career at the antipodes. Yet more—I, at least, can certify to this company that not such is the sense of public duty you inherited from your honored father, and have consistently illustrated throughout your own career. You will not fail, because you know the peril and the prize. You will not fail, because you have civilization and law and ordered freedom, the honor of your land and the happiness of a new one, in your care—because you know that, for uncounted peoples, the hopes of future years hang breathless on your fate. And so, gentlemen of the Commission, good-by, and God-speed!

In spite of rock and tempest's roar,

In spite of false lights on the shore,

Sail on, nor fear to breast the sea!

APPENDICES

1. Power to Acquire and Govern Territory.
2. The Tariff in United States Territory.
3. The Resolutions of Congress as to Cuba.
4. The Protocol of Washington.
5. The Peace of Paris.

1

POWER TO ACQUIRE AND GOVERN TERRITORY

The United States has as much power as any other Government.

"The Constitution of the United States established a Government, and not a league, compact, or partnership.... As a Government it was invested with all the attributes of sovereignty.... It is not only a Government, but it is a National Government, and the only Government in this country that has the character of nationality.... Such being the character of the General Government, it seems to be a self-evident proposition that it is invested with all those inherent and implied powers which, at the time of adopting the Constitution, were generally considered to belong to every Government as such, and as being essential to the exercise of its functions." (Mr. Justice Bradley, United States Supreme Court, Legal Tender Cases, 12 Wall. 554.)

The United States can acquire territory by conquest or by treaty, as a condition of peace or as indemnity.

"The United States ... may extend its boundaries by conquest or treaty, and may demand the cession of territory as the condition of peace, in order to indemnify its citizens for the injuries they have suffered, or to reimburse the Government for the expenses of the war. But this can only be done by the treaty-making power or the legislative authority." (United States Supreme Court, Fleming *et al.* *v.* Page, 9 How. 614.)

The United States can have a valid title by conquest to territory not a part of the Union.

"By the laws and usages of nations, conquest is a valid title.... As regarded by all other nations it [Tampico] was a part of the United States, and belonged to them as exclusively as a Territory included in our established boundaries, but yet it was not a part of the Union." (United States Supreme Court, Fleming *et al.* *v.* Page, 9 How. 603-615.)

A title so acquired by the United States cannot be questioned in its courts.

"If those departments which are intrusted with the foreign intercourse of the Nation ... have unequivocally asserted its rights of dominion over a country of which it is in possession and which it claims under a treaty, if the legislature has acted on the construction thus asserted, it is not in its own courts that this construction is to be denied. A question like this, respecting the boundaries of a nation, is ... more a political than a legal question, and in its discussion the courts of every country must respect the pronounced will of the legislature." (Mr. Chief Justice Marshall, Foster *et al. v.* Neilson, 2 Peters 253, 309.)

Yet such territory may be still outside the United States (meaning thereby the American Union organized by the Constitution—the Nation), *and cannot get in without action by the political authorities.*

"The boundaries of the United States, as they existed when war was declared against Mexico, were not extended by the conquest.... They remained unchanged. And every place which was out of the limits of the United States, as previously established by the political authorities of the Government, was still foreign." (Fleming *et al. v.* Page, 9 How. 616.)

The United States can govern such territory as it pleases. Thus it can withhold any power of local legislation.

"Possessing the power to erect a Territorial government for Alaska, they could confer upon it such powers, judicial and executive, as they deemed most suitable to the necessities of the inhabitants. It was unquestionably within the constitutional power of Congress to withhold from the inhabitants of Alaska the power to legislate and make laws. In the absence, then, of any law-making power in the Territory, to what source must the people look for the laws by which they are to be governed? This question can admit of but one answer. Congress is the only law-making power for Alaska." (United States *v.* Nelson, 29 Fed. Rep. 202, 205, 206.)

Mr. Jefferson even held that the United States could sell territory, hold it as a colony, or regulate its commerce as it pleased.

"The Territory [Louisiana] was purchased by the United States in their confederate capacity, and may be disposed of by them at their pleasure. It is in the nature of a colony whose commerce may be regulated without any reference to the Constitution." (And Louisiana was so governed for years after the purchase, with different tariff requirements from those of the United States, and without trial by jury in civil cases.)

Again, the United States may even (as in the case of Consular Courts) *withhold the right of trial by jury.*

"By the Constitution a government is ordained and established 'for the United States of America,' and not for countries outside of their limits. The guaranties it affords against accusation of capital or infamous crimes, except by indictment or presentment by a grand jury, and for an impartial trial by a jury when thus accused, apply only to citizens and others within the United States, or who are brought there for trial for alleged offenses committed elsewhere, and not to residents or temporary sojourners abroad. The Constitution can have no operation in another country." (*In re* Ross, 140 U.S. 463, 465.) (In this case the prisoner insisted that the refusal to allow him a trial by jury was a fatal defect in the jurisdiction exercised by the court, and rendered its judgment absolutely void.)

The United States can govern such territory through Congress.

"At the time the Constitution was formed the limits of the territory over which it was to operate were generally defined and recognized. These States, this territory, and future States to be admitted into the Union, are *the sole objects of the Constitution*. There is no express provision whatever made in the Constitution for the acquisition or government of territories beyond those limits. The right, therefore, of acquiring territory is altogether incidental to the treaty-making power, and perhaps to the power of admitting new States into the Union; and the government of such acquisitions is, of course, left to the legislative power of the Union, as far as that power is controlled by treaty." (Mr. Justice Johnson of the Supreme Court, sitting in the Circuit, in Am. Ins. Co. *v.* Canter, 1 Pet. 517.)

Mr. Chief Justice Marshall, affirming the above decision, says:

"Perhaps the power of governing a Territory belonging to the United States which has not, by becoming a State, acquired the means of self-government, may result necessarily from the facts that it is not within the jurisdiction of any particular State, and is within the power and jurisdiction of the United States. The right to govern may be the inevitable consequence of the right to acquire territory. Whichever may be the source whence the power is derived, the possession of it is unquestioned." (1 Pet. 541, 542.)

The General Government exercises a sovereignty independent of the Constitution.

"Their people [in organized Territories] do not constitute a sovereign power. All political authority exercised therein is derived [not from the Constitution, but] from the General Government." (Snow *v.* United States, 18 Wall. 317, 320.)

The General Government is expected, however, to be controlled as to personal and civil rights by the general principles of the Constitution.

"The personal and civil rights of the inhabitants of the Territories are secured to them, as to other citizens, by the principles of constitutional liberty which restrain all the agencies of government." (Murphy *v.* Ramsay, 114 U.S. 15, 44, 45.)

"Doubtless Congress, in legislating for the Territories, would be subject to those fundamental limitations in favor of personal rights which are formulated in the Constitution and its amendments; but these limitations would exist rather by inference and the general spirit of the Constitution, from which Congress derives all its powers, than by any express and direct application of its provisions." (Mormon Church *v.* United States, 136 U.S. 1, 44; Thompson *v.* Utah, 170 U.S. 343, 349.)

2

THE TARIFF IN UNITED STATES TERRITORY

The one point at which the opponents of the doctrine that Congress can govern the Territories as it pleases are able to make a prima facie case by quoting a decision of the Supreme Court, is as to the application of the United States tariff to the Territories. When California was acquired, but before Congress had acted or a Collection District had been established, the Supreme Court sustained the demand for duties under the United States tariff on goods landed at California ports (Cross *v.* Harrison, 16 How. 164). Mr. Justice Wayne said:

"By the ratifications of the treaty California became a part of the United States. And as there is nothing differently stipulated in the treaty with respect to commerce, it became instantly bound and privileged by the laws which Congress had passed to raise a revenue from duties on imports and tonnage.... The right claimed to land foreign goods within the United States at any place out of a Collection District, if allowed, would be a violation of that provision in the Constitution which enjoins that all duties, imposts, and excises shall be uniform throughout the United States."

The court here bases its reasoning distinctly on the treaty by which California was acquired. But that treaty gave the pledge that California (an adjacent Territory) should be incorporated into the American Union. The Treaty of Paris gave no such pledge as to the Philippines (not adjacent territory, but nine thousand miles away), could not in the nature of the case have given such a pledge, and did provide, instead, that the whole question of the civil rights and political status of the native inhabitants should be determined by the Congress. Recalling Mr. Justice Story's remark that in a Constitution "there ought to be a capacity to provide for future contingencies as they may happen, and as these are ... illimitable in their nature, so it is impossible safely to limit that capacity," it would seem that there would certainly be elasticity enough in the Constitution, or common sense enough in its interpretation, to permit the Supreme Court to perceive some difference between a requirement of uniform tariff on this continent over a territory specifically acquired in order to be made a State, and such a requirement on the other side of the globe over territory not so acquired. The case becomes stronger when the treaty (also constitutionally a part of the Supreme Law of the land) turns over the political status of the latter territory entirely to Congress.

The Constitution makes the same or similar requirements of uniformity throughout the United States as to the tariff, internal taxes, courts, and the right of trial by jury. But in every case the early practice did not construe this to include the Territories.

As to uniformity in tariff. It was not enforced rigidly in Louisiana for years. So little, in fact, was it then held that Louisiana, as soon as acquired, became an integral part of the United States (notwithstanding the treaty provision that in time it should), that though the directors of the United States Bank were empowered to establish offices of discount and deposit "wheresoever they shall think fit *within the United States,*" they did not consider this a warrant for establishing one in New Orleans, and actually secured from the Congress for that purpose a bill, signed by Thomas Jefferson on March 23, 1804, extending their authority, under the terms of their original charter, to "any part of the Territories or dependencies of the United States."

As to uniformity in internal taxes. The very first levied in the United States, that of March 3, 1791, omitted the Territories altogether, dividing the United States into fourteen Collection Districts, "each consisting of one State." It is not until 1798 that any trace can be found of a collection of internal revenue in the territory northwest of the Ohio.

As to the courts. The Constitution requires that the judicial officers of the United States shall hold office during good behavior. For a century the judicial officers of Territories have been restricted to fixed terms of office.

As to trial by jury. The Constitution gives the right to it to every criminal case in the United States, and to every civil case involving over twenty dollars. Under Mr. Jefferson's government of Louisiana, trial by jury was limited to capital cases in criminal prosecutions. It has likewise been denied in Consular Courts.

3

THE RESOLUTIONS OF CONGRESS AS TO CUBA

Adopted by Congress, April 19, 1898: by the Senate at 1:38 a.m., 42 to 35; by the House at 2:40 a.m., 311 to 6.

Whereas, The abhorrent conditions which have existed for more than three years in the island of Cuba, so near our own borders, have shocked the moral sense of the people of the United States, have been a disgrace to Christian civilization,—culminating, as they have, in the destruction of a United States battle-ship, with two hundred and sixty of its officers and crew, while on a friendly visit in the harbor of Havana,—and cannot longer be endured, as has been set forth by the President of the United States in his message to Congress of April 11, 1898, upon which the action of Congress was invited; therefore be it resolved,

First, That the people of the island of Cuba are, and of right ought to be, free and independent.

Second, That it is the duty of the United States to demand, and the Government of the United States does hereby demand, that the Government of Spain at once relinquish its authority and government in the island of Cuba and withdraw its land and naval forces from Cuba and Cuban waters.

Third, That the President of the United States be, and he hereby is, directed and empowered to use the entire land and naval forces of the United States, and to call into the actual service of the United States the militia of the several States to such an extent as may be necessary to carry these resolutions into effect.

Fourth, That the United States hereby disclaims any disposition or intention to exercise sovereignty, jurisdiction, or control over said island, except for the pacification thereof, and asserts its determination when that is accomplished to leave the government and control of the island to its people.

4

THE PROTOCOL OF WASHINGTON

William R. Day, Secretary of State of the United States, and His Excellency Jules Cambon, Ambassador Extraordinary and Plenipotentiary of the Republic of France at Washington, respectively possessing for this purpose full authority from the Government of the United States and the Government of Spain, have concluded and signed the following articles, embodying the terms on which the two Governments have agreed in respect to the matters hereinafter set forth, having in view the establishment of peace between the two countries, that is to say:

Article I

Spain will relinquish all claim of sovereignty over and title to Cuba.

Article II

Spain will cede to the United States the island of Porto Rico and other islands now under Spanish sovereignty in the West Indies, and also an island in the Ladrones to be selected by the United States.

Article III

The United States will occupy and hold the city, bay, and harbor of Manila, pending the conclusion of a treaty of peace which shall determine the control, disposition, and government of the Philippines.

Article IV

Spain will immediately evacuate Cuba, Porto Rico, and other islands now under Spanish sovereignty in the West Indies; and to this end each Government will, within ten days after the signing of this protocol, appoint Commissioners, and the Commissioners so appointed shall, within thirty days after the signing of this protocol, meet at Havana for the purpose of arranging and carrying out the details of the aforesaid evacuation of Cuba and the adjacent Spanish islands; and each Government will, within ten days after the signing of this protocol, also appoint other Commissioners, who shall, within thirty days after the signing of this protocol, meet at San Juan, in Porto Rico, for the purpose of arranging and carrying out the details of the aforesaid evacuation of Porto Rico and other islands now under Spanish sovereignty in the West Indies.

Article V

The United States and Spain will each appoint not more than five Commissioners to treat of peace, and the Commissioners so appointed shall meet at Paris not later than October 1, 1898, and proceed to the negotiation and conclusion of a treaty of peace, which treaty shall be subject to ratification according to the respective constitutional forms of the two countries.

Article VI

Upon the conclusion and signing of this protocol, hostilities between the two countries shall be suspended, and notice to that effect shall be given as soon as possible by each Government to the commanders of its military and naval forces.

Done at Washington in duplicate, in English and in French, by the undersigned, who have hereunto set their hands and seals the twelfth day of August, 1898.

- (Seal) William R. Day.
- (Seal) Jules Cambon.

5

THE PEACE OF PARIS

Negotiations begun in Paris, October 1, 1898. Treaty signed in Paris, 8:45 p.m., December 10. Delivered by United States Commissioners to the President, December 24; transmitted to the Senate with the official report of the negotiations, January 4, 1899; ratified by Senate in executive session, February 6, by a vote of 57 against 27. Formal exchange of ratifications at Washington, April 11. Twenty millions paid through Jules Cambon, May 1. Treaty ratified by Spanish Senate, July 3, 1899.

The United States of America and Her Majesty the Queen Regent of Spain, in the name of her august son, Don Alfonso XIII, desiring to end the state of war now existing between the two countries, have for that purpose appointed as plenipotentiaries:

The President of the United States,

William R. Day, Cushman K. Davis, William P. Frye, George Gray, and Whitelaw Reid, citizens of the United States;

And Her Majesty the Queen Regent of Spain,

Don Eugenio Montero Rios, President of the Senate; Don Buenaventura de Abarzuza, Senator of the Kingdom and ex-Minister of the Crown; Don Jose de Garnica, Deputy to the Cortes and Associate Justice of the Supreme Court; Don Wenceslao Ramirez de Villa Urrutia, Envoy Extraordinary and Minister Plenipotentiary at Brussels; and Don Rafael Cerero, General of Division;

Who, having assembled in Paris and having exchanged their full powers, which were found to be in due and proper form, have, after discussion of the matters before them, agreed upon the following articles:

Article I. Spain relinquishes all claim of sovereignty over and title to Cuba.

And as the island is, upon its evacuation by Spain, to be occupied by the United States, the United States will, so long as such occupation shall last, assume and discharge the obligations that may under international law result from the fact of its occupation for the protection of life and property.

Article II. Spain cedes to the United States the island of Porto Rico and other islands now under Spanish sovereignty in the West Indies, and the island of Guam, in the Marianas or Ladrones.

Article III. Spain cedes to the United States the archipelago known as the Philippine Islands, and comprehending the islands lying within the following lines:

A line running from west to east along or near the twentieth parallel of north latitude, and through the middle of the navigable channel of Bachti, from the one hundred and eighteenth (118th) to the one hundred and twenty-seventh (127th) degree meridian of longitude east of Greenwich, thence along the one hundred and twenty-seventh (127th) degree meridian of longitude east of Greenwich to the parallel of four degrees and forty-five minutes (4° 45′) north latitude, thence along the parallel of four degrees and forty-five minutes (4° 45′) north latitude to its intersection with the meridian of longitude one hundred and nineteen degrees and thirty-five minutes (119° 35′) east of Greenwich, thence along the meridian of longitude one hundred and nineteen degrees and thirty-five minutes (119° 35′) east of Greenwich to the parallel of latitude seven degrees and forty minutes (7° 40′) north, thence along the parallel of latitude seven degrees and forty minutes (7° 40′) north to its intersection with the one hundred and sixteenth (116th) degree meridian of longitude east of Greenwich, thence by a direct line to the intersection of the tenth (10th) degree parallel of north latitude with the one hundred and eighteenth (118th) degree meridian of longitude east of Greenwich, and thence along the one hundred and eighteenth (118th) degree meridian of longitude east of Greenwich to the point of beginning.

The United States will pay to Spain the sum of twenty million dollars ($20,000,000) within three months after the exchange of the ratifications of the present treaty.

Article IV. The United States will for ten years from the date of exchange of ratifications of the present treaty admit Spanish ships and merchandise to the ports of the Philippine Islands on the same terms as ships and merchandise of the United States.

Article V. The United States will, upon the signature of the present treaty, send back to Spain, at its own cost, the Spanish soldiers taken as prisoners of war on the capture of Manila by the American forces. The arms of the soldiers in question shall be restored to them.

Spain will, upon the exchange of the ratifications of the present treaty, proceed to evacuate the Philippines, as well as the island of Guam, on terms similar to those agreed upon by the Commissioners appointed to arrange for the evacuation of Porto Rico and other islands in the West Indies under the protocol of August 12, 1898, which is to continue in force till its provisions are completely executed.

The time within which the evacuation of the Philippine Islands and Guam shall be completed shall be fixed by the two Governments. Stands of colors, uncaptured war-vessels, small arms, guns of all calibers, with their carriages and accessories, powder, ammunition, live stock, and materials and supplies of all kinds belonging to the land and naval forces of Spain in the Philippines and Guam remain the property of Spain. Pieces of heavy ordnance, exclusive of field artillery, in the fortifications and coast defenses, shall remain in their emplacements for the term of six months, to be reckoned from the exchange of ratifications of the treaty; and the United States may in the meantime purchase such material from Spain, if a satisfactory agreement between the two Governments on the subject shall be reached.

Article VI. Spain will, upon the signature of the present treaty, release all prisoners of war and all persons detained or imprisoned for political offenses in connection with the insurrections in Cuba and the Philippines and the war with the United States.

Reciprocally the United States will release all persons made prisoners of war by the American forces, and will undertake to obtain the release of all Spanish prisoners in the hands of the insurgents in Cuba and the Philippines.

The Government of the United States will at its own cost return to Spain, and the Government of Spain will at its own cost return to the United States, Cuba, Porto Rico, and the Philippines, according to the situation of their respective homes, prisoners released or caused to be released by them, respectively, under this article.

Article VII. The United States and Spain mutually relinquish all claims for indemnity, national and individual, of every kind, of either Government, or of its citizens or subjects, against the other Government, which may have arisen since the beginning of the late insurrection in Cuba, and prior to the exchange of ratifications of the present treaty, including all claims for indemnity for the cost of the war. The United States will adjudicate and settle the claims of its citizens against Spain relinquished in this article.

Article VIII. In conformity with the provisions of Articles I, II, and III of this treaty, Spain relinquishes in Cuba and cedes in Porto Rico and other islands in the West Indies, in the island of Guam, and in the Philippine Archipelago all the buildings, wharves, barracks, forts, structures, public highways, and other immovable property which in conformity with law belong to the public domain and as such belong to the Crown of Spain.

And it is hereby declared that the relinquishment or cession, as the case may be, to which the preceding paragraph refers, cannot in any respect impair the property or rights which by law belong to the peaceful possession of property of all kinds of provinces, municipalities, public or private establishments, ecclesiastical or civic bodies or any other associations having legal capacity to acquire and possess property in the aforesaid territories renounced or ceded, or of private individuals, of whatsoever nationality such individuals may be.

The aforesaid relinquishment or cession, as the case may be, includes all documents exclusively referring to the sovereignty relinquished or ceded that may exist in the archives of the Peninsula. Where any document in such archives only in part relates to said sovereignty a copy of such part will be furnished whenever it shall be requested. Like rules shall be reciprocally observed in favor of Spain in respect of documents in the archives of the islands above referred to.

In the aforesaid relinquishment or cession, as the case may be, are also included such rights as the Crown of Spain and its authorities possess in respect of the official archives and records, executive as well as judicial, in the islands above referred to, which relate to said islands or the rights and property of their inhabitants. Such archives and records shall be carefully preserved, and private persons shall, without distinction, have the right to require, in accordance with the law, authenticated copies of the contracts, wills, and other instruments forming pact of notarial protocols or files, or which may be contained in the executive or judicial archives, be the latter in Spain or in the islands aforesaid.

Article IX. Spanish subjects, natives of the Peninsula, residing in the territory over which Spain by the present treaty relinquishes or cedes her sovereignty, may remain in such territory or may remove therefrom, retaining in either event all their rights of property, including the right to sell or dispose of such property or of its proceeds; and they shall also have the right to carry on their industry, commerce, and professions, being subject in respect thereof to such laws as are applicable to other foreigners. In case they remain in the territory they may preserve their allegiance to the Crown of Spain by making, before a court of record, within a year from the date of the exchange of ratifications of this treaty, a declaration of their decision to preserve such allegiance; in default of which declaration they shall be held to have renounced it and to have adopted the nationality of the territory in which they may reside.

The civil rights and political status of the native inhabitants of the territories hereby ceded to the United States shall be determined by the Congress.

Article X. The inhabitants of the territories over which Spain relinquishes or cedes her sovereignty shall be secured in the free exercise of their religion.

Article XI. The Spaniards residing in the territories over which Spain by this treaty cedes or relinquishes her sovereignty shall be subject in matters civil as well as criminal to the jurisdiction of the courts of the country wherein they reside, pursuant to the ordinary laws governing the same; and they shall have the right to appear before such courts and to pursue the same course as citizens of the country to which the courts belong.

Article XII. Judicial proceedings pending at the time of the exchange of ratifications of this treaty in the territories over which Spain relinquishes or cedes her sovereignty shall be determined according to the following rules:

First. Judgments rendered either in civil suits between private individuals or in criminal matters, before the date mentioned, and with respect to which there is no recourse or right of review under the Spanish law, shall be deemed to be final, and shall be executed in due form by competent authority in the territory within which such judgments should be carried out.

Second. Civil suits between private individuals which may on the date mentioned be undetermined shall be prosecuted to judgment before the court in which they may then be pending, or in the court that may be substituted therefor.

Third. Criminal actions pending on the date mentioned before the Supreme Court of Spain against citizens of the territory which by this treaty ceases to be Spanish shall continue under its jurisdiction until final judgment; but, such judgment having been rendered, the execution thereof shall be committed to the competent authority of the place in which the case arose.

Article XIII. The rights of property secured by copyrights and patents acquired by Spaniards in the island of Cuba, and in Porto Rico, the Philippines, and other ceded territories, at the time of the exchange of the ratifications of this treaty, shall continue to be respected. Spanish scientific, literary, and artistic works not subversive of public order in the territories in question shall continue to be admitted free of duty into such territories for the period of ten years, to be reckoned from the date of the exchange of the ratifications of this treaty.

Article XIV. Spain shall have the power to establish consular officers in the ports and places of the territories the sovereignty over which has either been relinquished or ceded by the present treaty.

Article XV. The Government of each country will, for the term of ten years, accord to the merchant-vessels of the other country the same treatment in respect to all port charges, including entrance and clearance dues, light dues and tonnage duties, as it accords to its own merchant-vessels not engaged in the coastwise trade.

This article may at any time be terminated on six months' notice given by either Government to the other.

Article XVI. It is understood that any obligations assumed in this treaty by the United States with respect to Cuba are limited to the time of its occupancy thereof; but it will, upon the termination of such occupancy, advise any Government established in the island to assume the same obligations.

Article XVII. The present treaty shall be ratified by the President of the United States, by and with the advice and consent of the Senate thereof, and by Her Majesty the Queen Regent of Spain; and the ratifications shall be exchanged at Washington within six months from the date hereof, or earlier if possible.

In faith whereof we, the respective plenipotentiaries, have signed this treaty and have hereunto affixed our seals.

Done in duplicate at Paris, the tenth day of December, in the year of our Lord one thousand eight hundred and ninety-eight.

- (Seal) William R. Day.
- (Seal) Cushman K. Davis.
- (Seal) William P. Frye.
- (Seal) George Gray.
- (Seal) Whitelaw Reid.
- (Seal) Eugenio Montero Rios.
- (Seal) B. de Abarzuza.
- (Seal) J. de Garnica.
- (Seal) W. R. de Villa Urrutia.
- (Seal) Rafael Cerero.

Footnotes

[1] At this time it was still a secret that among the many intrigues afoot during the negotiations at Paris was one for the transfer of the Philippines to Belgium. But for the perfectly correct attitude of King Leopold, it might have had a chance to succeed, or at least to make trouble.

[2] The request of the editor for the preparation of this article was received just after the British and American forces had their conflict with the natives in Samoa.

[3] One of the author's colleagues at Paris, the Hon. Cushman K. Davis, chairman of the Foreign Relations Committee of the United States Senate, and among the most scholarly students of International Law now in American public life, says in a private letter:

"I was at first very much struck by the unanimity of action by the South American republics in the assumption of debts created by Spain. But some reflection upon the subject has caused that action to lose, to me, much of its apparent relevancy. There was in none of those cases any funded debt, in the sense of bond obligations, held in the markets of the world. There were two parties in the various Spanish provinces of North and South America, one of which supported Spanish ascendancy, and the other of which was revolutionary. The debts created by the exactions of Spain and of the revolutionary party alike were, mainly if not entirely, obligations due to the people of the colonies themselves. As to the continuance of pensions, endowments, etc., it must be remembered that these were Catholic countries, and that these obligations ran to a state church, which continued to be a state church after the colonies had achieved their independence. As to the Napoleonic treaties cited by the Spanish Commissioners, they were mere matters of covenant in a special case, and were not, in my judgment, the result of any anterior national obligation."]

[4] It might, of course, have run away and left them to disorder. That is what a pirate could have done, and would have compelled the intervention of European governments for the protection of their own citizens. Or it might have restored them to Spain. Besides the desertion of natives whose aid against Manila had been encouraged, that would have been to say that while the United States went to war because the injustice and barbarity of Spanish rule in the West Indies were such that they could no longer be tolerated, it was now so eager to quit and get peace that it was willing to reëstablish that same rule in the East Indies!

[5] Much attention had been attracted, as the date for this celebration approached, to the numerous sons of this small college who had in one way or another become prominent; and the newspapers printed long lists of them. Among the names thus singled out in the press were Benjamin Harrison, of the class of 1852, President of the United States, 1889-93; William Dennison, class of 1835, Governor of Ohio, 1859-63, and Postmaster-General under Abraham Lincoln;

Caleb B. Smith, 1826, Secretary of the Interior in the same Administration; General Robert C. Schenck, 1827, Chairman Ways and Means Committee in House of Representatives, Major-General in the Civil War, and United States Minister to Brazil and to Great Britain; William S. Groesbeck, 1834, Congressman, counsel for Andrew Johnson in the impeachment proceedings, and United States delegate to the International Monetary Congress, 1878; Samuel Shellabarger, 1841, Congressman, member of the Crédit Mobilier Investigation, and of the United States Civil Service Commission; Oliver P. Morton, 1845, War Governor of Indiana, and United States Senator; Charles Anderson, 1833, Governor of Ohio; James Birney, 1836, Governor of Michigan; Richard Yates, 1830, War Governor of Illinois, and United States Senator; Milton Sayler, 1852, Speaker House of Representatives; John S. Williams, 1838, the "Cerro Gordo Williams" of the Mexican War, United States Senator from Kentucky; George E. Pugh, 1840, United States Senator from Ohio; James W. McDill, 1853, United States Senator from Iowa; General Samuel F. Carey, 1835, Congressman from Ohio, and temperance orator; Albert S. Berry, 1856, Congressman from Kentucky; Dr. John S. Billings, U.S.A., 1857, head of New York Library; David Swing, 1852, the Chicago clergyman; General A. C. McClurg, 1853, the Chicago publisher; Henry M. MacCracken, 1857, Chancellor of New York University; William M. Thomson, 1828, author of "The Land and the Book"; Calvin S. Brice, 1863, railway-builder, and United States Senator; etc.

[6] "My dear Sir: I have received your letter of the 23d inst., notifying me of my election as a vice-president of the Anti-Imperialist League. I recognize the compliment implied in this election, and appreciate it the more by reason of my respect for the gentlemen identified with the league, but I do not think I can appropriately or consistently accept the position, especially since I learn through the press that the league adopted at its recent meeting certain resolutions to which I cannot assent.... I may add that, while I fully recognize the injustice and even absurdity of those charges of 'disloyalty' which have been of late freely made against some members of the league, and also that many honorable and patriotic men do not feel as I do on this subject, I am personally unwilling to take part in an agitation which may have some tendency to cause a public enemy

to persist in armed resistance, or may be, at least, plausibly represented as having this tendency. There can be no doubt that, as a matter of fact, the country is at war with Aguinaldo and his followers. I profoundly regret this fact;... but it is a fact, nevertheless, and, as such, must weigh in determining my conduct as a citizen....

"Charles Jerome Bonaparte.

"Baltimore,
"May 25, 1899."

[7] The Hon. Albert S. Berry, M.C., from the Covington, Kentucky, District.

[8] Protocol No. 19 of the Paris Commission, Conference of December 5, 1898: "The President of the Spanish Commission having agreed, at the last session, to consult his Government regarding the proposal of the American Commissioners that the United States should maintain public order over the whole Philippine Archipelago pending the exchange of ratifications of the treaty of peace, stated that the answer of his Government was that the authorities of each of the two nations shall be charged with the maintenance of order in the places where they may be established, those authorities agreeing among themselves to this end whenever they may deem it necessary."

[9] Some of these authorities have already been briefly presented in the address at Miami University, pp. 107-158. It may be desirable to consult a few additional ones, covering the main points that have been disputed. They are grouped for convenience in the Appendix.

[10] London "Times," December 17, 1898.

[11] See (pp. 70-105) article from "The Anglo-Saxon Review."

[12] There has been so much misconception and misrepresentation about this payment of twenty millions that the following exact summary of the facts may be convenient.

When Spain sued for peace in the summer of 1898, she had lost control of the Philippines, and any means for regaining control. Her fleet was sunk; her army was cooped up in the capital, under the guns of the American fleet, and its capture or surrender had only been delayed till the arrival of reinforcements for the American Army, because of the fears expressed by foreigners and the principal residents of Manila that the city might be looted by natives unless American land forces were at hand in strength ample to control them. The Spanish army did so surrender, in fact, shortly after the arrival of these reinforcements, before the news of the armistice could reach them.

In the protocol granting an armistice, the United States exacted at once the cession of Porto Rico and an island in the Ladrones, but reserved the decision as to the control, disposition, and government of the Philippines for the treaty of peace, apparently with a view to the possibility of accepting them as further indemnity for the war.

When the treaty came to be negotiated, the United States required the cession of the Philippines. Its Peace Commissioners stated that their Government "felt amply supported in its right to demand this cession, with or without concessions," added that "this demand might be limited to the single ground of indemnity," and pointed out that it was "not now putting forward any claim for *pecuniary* indemnity, to cover the enormous cost of the war." It accompanied this demand for a transfer of sovereignty with a stipulation for assuming any existing indebtedness of Spain incurred for public works and improvements of a pacific character in the Philippines. The United States thus asserted its right to the archipelago for indemnity, and at the same time committed itself to the principle of payment on account of the Philippine debt.

When it became necessary to put the Philippine case into an ultimatum, the Peace Commissioners did not further refer to the debt or give any specific reason either for a cession or for a payment. They simply said they now presented "a new proposition, embodying the concessions which, for the sake of immediate peace, their Government is, under the circumstances, willing to tender."

But it was really the old proposition (with the "Open Door" and "Mutual Relinquishment of Claims" clauses added), with the mention for the first time of a specific sum for the payment, and without any question of "pacific improvements." That sum just balanced the Philippine debt—40,000,000 Mexican, or, say, 20,000,000 American dollars.

13 General Carl Schurz, at the Chicago Anti-Expansion Convention, October, 1899.

14 The exact proposition made by General Carl Schurz in addressing the Chicago Anti-Expansion Convention, October 17, 1899.

15 General Carl Schurz, at the Philadelphia Anti-Imperialist Convention, February 22, 1900.

16 Thomas Corwin of Ohio, in United States Senate, 1848.

17 Over a month after the above was delivered came the first recent judicial expression of a contrary view. It was by Judge William Lochren of the United States Circuit Court at St. Paul, in the case of habeas corpus proceedings against Reeve, warden of the Minnesota State Prison at Stillwater, for the release of a Porto Rican named Ortiz. He was held for the murder of a private soldier of the United States, sentenced to death by a Military Commission at San Juan, and, on commutation of the sentence by the President of the United States, sent to this State Prison for life. Judge Lochren denied the writ on the ground that the conviction took place before the Treaty of Paris, by which Spain ceded sovereignty in Porto Rico to the United States, had been ratified by the Senate. The Judge went on, however, to argue that Ortiz could not have been lawfully tried before the Military Commission after the ratification of the treaty,

because the island of Porto Rico thereby became an integral part of the United States, subject to the Constitution and privileged and bound by its provisions. As this point was not involved in the case he was deciding, this is, of course, merely a dictum—the expression of opinion on an outside matter by a Democratic judge who was recently transferred by Mr. Cleveland from a Washington bureau to the bench. It clearly shows, however, what would be his decision whenever the case might come before him. His argument followed closely the lines taken by Mr. Calhoun in the Senate and Mr. Chief Justice Taney in the Dred Scott decision.